The Art of Elementary Band Directing

EILEEN FRAEDRICH

MEREDITH MUSIC PUBLICATIONS

Published By

MEREDITH MUSIC PUBLICATIONS

a division of G.W. Music, Inc.

MEREDITH MUSIC PUBLICATIONS and its stylized double M logo are trademarks
of Meredith Music Publications, a division of G.W. Music, Inc.

Book design and layout by Shawn Brown
Cover design by John Heinly

ISBN: 1-57463-053-9

Second Edition
September 2003

Table of Contents

Introduction

All beginning teachers face many challenges in their first year on the job; beginning band teachers are no exception. In that year, they learn more about teaching than they do in all of their years of preparation. Much of their knowledge is acquired through trial and error. Years later they think, "If only I had known then what I know now..."

Although many fine instrumental pedagogy books have been published, little has been written on the art of teaching elementary band—and it is an art. It is also a business. The elementary band director must be a teacher, a salesperson, a politician, a psychologist, an economist, a writer, an editor, an instrument repairman, and a musician rolled into one. There is much more to the profession than merely teaching the skills of music to children; before the teaching can even begin, the aspiring band director must don many hats.

With this in mind, I have created a handbook for the beginning band teacher. It thoroughly covers the managerial aspects of operating an elementary band program from recruitment to method book selection to concert preparation. As a 1991 Teacher of the Year Nominee and former director of the largest elementary band program in Fairfax County, Virginia, I believe that I have much useful information to share. I hope that this handbook will enable new teachers to benefit from my teaching experience.

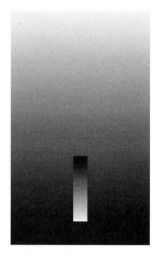

The Successful Recruitment Program

Asuccessful band recruitment campaign is perhaps the single most important step toward building a strong elementary band program; before one can begin to teach, one must first have students. The elementary band director who wishes to build a band must be at least as good at salesmanship as at musicianship. The fervor and zeal with which the director approaches the recruitment process directly affect student response and, consequently, the overall band program. The following is a guide to the recruitment process:

As early as possible in the school year, set up times for the recruitment (band instrument demonstration) assembly with the classroom teachers. Having an assembly sometime the first week is ideal—interest and enthusiasm are high, and students have not yet become committed to too many other activities which are newly available to them. I have found that an assembly for each grade level works well. If you have over 150 students in a grade, you may want to split them up into smaller groups and have additional assemblies.

You will need a large room for this assembly—remember to sign up in advance for the room you will be using. If using the cafeteria, check with the food service and custodial staffs to be sure that noisy machinery (dishwasher, vacuum) will be silent during your program.

PREPARATION
Set A Program
Date And Place

Some directors prefer to do a smaller presentation in the more intimate setting of the classroom. A smaller group facilitates the passing around of instruments, an important step to recruitment. The informal atmosphere is appealing; however, I view the recruitment assembly as a grand show and prefer to make it a special event to which the students look forward. Only you can decide what approach will work best in your school.

Arrange For Instrument Demonstrations

The primary part of an elementary band recruitment assembly is the demonstration of all band instruments. This is a director's opportunity to make or break the band program for the entire year. Students will not sign up to play instruments which they have never heard; consequently, unless enlightened by the band director, most students tend to go for the popular instrument choices—flute, trumpet, saxophone, and drums. The result is a poorly balanced, trebly band which will weaken the elementary, junior high, and high school pyramid for the next eight years. The solution is to have a desired instrumentation in mind, to demonstrate and discuss all instruments, and to devote the greatest amount of time and attention to those instruments that are less popular but so necessary for a properly balanced band—tuba, baritone, trombone, French horn, and oboe.

There are several approaches to instrument demonstration: the band director may personally demonstrate all instruments, high school students in the pyramid may demonstrate, or sixth-grade, second-year students may demonstrate. The latter is my preferred choice for many reasons: students in the audience identify with the performers and can get an idea of what they might sound like in a year; the returning second-year students are motivated by the chance to perform, and this starts the year off well; and students may join together as a mini-band to play an effective grand finale. Some directors prefer to involve high school students since they should perform better than elementary students. The performance can be particularly effective when the high school musicians come dressed in full marching band uniform; however, scheduling difficulties arise since these students would either need to miss school or the assembly would have to be scheduled at the end of the day, after the high school has been dismissed.

If you decide to have sixth graders demonstrate, you will need to give them the musical excerpts to perform and you will need to set up a rehearsal time. This preparation must be done during the first day or two of school if you intend to have an assembly by the end of the first week. It may be wise to contact students before school starts. If this is your first year at the school, you will need guidance in selecting demonstrators. If the previous band director is available, you may wish to ask for a recommendation. The general music teacher often knows the musically strong students and can offer suggestions.

The selection of musical excerpts for demonstration is an important facet of a band recruitment program—I have known students to select their instrument based on their preference for a song that was demonstrated. Give some thought to what would appeal to students. A pop tune, a folk song, or a television theme might be good choices. I recall that one year I played a short snake-charmer tune on the oboe and the students loved it; that year I had an overwhelming number of oboe students. If you are hoping to increase your enrollment numbers on a particular instrument, choose a piece which will best show it off.

Select Music For Demonstration

In advance of the recruitment program, you will need to prepare a letter to go home with students. The letter will be representing you to the parents; it should be inviting, professional, and letter-perfect. The following information should be included:

Prepare A Recruitment Letter

- Mention the role of band in the curriculum at all levels
- Describe your band program—frequency and composition of classes, goals, performance opportunities
- Inform parents about instrument rental
- Discuss the parents' informational meeting
- Include a portion of the form to be returned if interested

Submit the letter for the principal's approval far enough in advance to allow time to make necessary changes and to run off copies. Clip-Art books and computer programs are available commercially and can be used to add to a letter's appeal. (See sample recruitment letter—Appendix A.)

Following the recruitment assembly, it is wise to hold an informational meeting for parents of interested band students. The date should be set and marked on the school calendar as soon as possible. Scheduling the meeting approximately one week after the recruitment program is suggested as this allows time to follow up the assembly with classroom visits.

Set A Date For A Parents' Informational Meeting

Prepare a reminder flyer to be sent home with students on the day of the informational meeting. (See sample parents' meeting reminder notice—Appendix B.)

Begin Aptitude Testing

While I do not use aptitude testing in my program, it is commonly used by many directors. There are a few standardized tests which are available. These tests identify students who demonstrate high levels of musical ability. The director can then use this information to make decisions regarding student participation and choice of instrument.

THE RECRUITMENT PROGRAM
Set The Mood

Try to create an air of festivity as classes arrive for the assembly. Sousa marches piped into the hallway and some colorful band posters placed at strategic spots leading toward the assembly can enhance student anticipation. An eye-catching display of instruments, placed in a prominent location, can further create interest. Your local music store may be willing to loan you shiny new instruments for this purpose.

Put On A Show

Once all classes have arrived, begin the program. Thirty-five to forty-five minutes should be sufficient for the assembly. The following is a suggested program order:

1. Introduce yourself
2. Briefly discuss the band program
   - as 5th/6th graders, students are eligible
   - no tuition is charged/books are provided
   - no music background is necessary
   - classes are held during school
   - instruments can be rented at a low cost
3. Do instrument demonstrations

I like to have student demonstrators seated up front, in score order (highest to lowest pitched instruments): flute, clarinet, oboe, saxophone, trumpet, French horn, trombone, baritone, tuba, percussion. This placement allows the audience to see and hear the instruments in relation to each other.

As each instrument is introduced, tell students a little bit about it (i.e., "The flute is the highest pitched instrument in our band" or "If I uncoiled the French horn, it would stretch all the way across the front of the room.") There are many instrument "fun facts" to share with students; they are often fascinated by what would perhaps seem insignificant to professional musicians. Pass around a clarinet or saxophone reed and show them that the instrument will not play without this small piece—they will be awed. Involve the audience in the program by asking questions and calling for volunteers (i.e., "How many of you have ever tried blowing across the top of a soda bottle to make a sound? That is the way we blow the flute" or "All brass instruments are played by buzzing into a mouthpiece like this—buzz. Let's see who can do that.")

Students love to come up and hold an instrument. I often give students the "trombone test," asking for a volunteer from the audience. I show the student how to hold the instrument, and I tell the audience that people often wonder how a trombone player knows where to move the slide for different notes since there are no markings to follow. I tell them that there are seven slide positions (or places to stop the slide) on the trombone and that we can get out more than one note for each position. Then I show them where first and third positions are (easy to see since the slide grip is either up against the stop or nearly even with the bell), and I ask them to take a guess as to where second position would be. Most students realize that this is halfway between first and third, and they enjoy moving the slide to the new position. Be prepared to have everyone in the audience begging to be called upon to try this.

4. Pass out the informational letter and go over its contents
5. Tell students about the parents' informational meeting
6. Answer questions

Some of the most frequently asked questions are listed below. Know in advance how you will respond.

- How much does it cost?
- Which instrument is the cheapest?
- What if I can't read music?
- Can you play in both band and strings?
- What if I want to quit?
- What subject will you pull me out of?

Many students are extremely concerned about the cost of renting instruments; they select an instrument based on rental price rather than on personal preference because they believe that their parents would be more agreeable to a less expensive instrument. I answer the students' questions regarding cost, but I try not to get stuck on this issue because it can usurp the program. Most instruments rent for moderate monthly fees through the local music stores in Fairfax County and for less through the schools; while fees may seem expensive to students, parents generally find them acceptable. I suggest that the students choose an instrument that they like and allow adults to discuss cost and finally decide.

7. Pass around instruments

Be sure to budget time for this final important activity. Children love to see the instruments up close, to push the valves and keys, and to move the slides. I suggest removing mouthpieces from the instruments before passing them. This eliminates the overwhelming temptation of students to blow the instruments.

FOLLOW-UP
Visit Classrooms

During the week between the recruitment program and the parents' meeting, visit the classrooms as often as possible. Times can be arranged with classroom teachers in advance. Take extra informational letters with you because students frequently misplace theirs. Remind students of the parents' meeting and be prepared to answer a myriad of questions with each visit. Carrying an instrument or two with you on these visits is an effective method for generating interest. Students will want to handle the instruments and will look forward to seeing more instruments on your next visit.

Pass Out Parents' Meeting Reminder Notices

On the day of the parents' meeting, pass out reminder notices and have the meeting announced. If you are responsible for several different elementary schools, leave notices at each school in advance.

Administer Any Music Aptitude Tests

Use your judgment in handling testing: fear of failing a test may turn off potentially good students, jeopardizing your recruitment.

Become A Familiar Face

Make your presence known in the school. Visit the cafeteria when the upper grades are eating lunch; talk to students. Volunteer for morning or afternoon hall duty or bus duty. Keep a high profile!

SUMMARY

The elementary band recruitment program determines the band's enrollment for the year. When trying to build a strong band program, you first need a large enrollment. The recruitment program should be approached with all of the creativity, enthusiasm, and energy that a band director can muster. ■

The Parents' Informational Meeting

The parents' meeting is, in many ways, a repeat of the student recruitment program. You must sell yourself and the band program. Be professional, positive, confident, respectful and honest. Convey your enthusiasm and competence. Show parents that their children will benefit from your teaching. At this meeting, instruments should be demonstrated and information should be discussed in detail.

PREPARATION

Prepare a parents' meeting reminder letter to go home with students on the day of the meeting. Include in that letter the date, time and location of the event. If you will be using student demonstrators, which I have found parents to greatly enjoy and appreciate since it gives them an idea of how their children may be playing in a year, make arrangements with their parents either over the phone, in person or in writing. Specify what you would like the students to wear and when they should arrive.

Set the mood for the meeting by preparing the room. Many of the suggestions given for the recruitment program also apply for the parents' meeting. Have all instruments on display—again, your local music store may be willing to loan you shiny new instruments for this purpose. Include all required accessories in your instrument display (reeds, neck straps, cork grease, valve oil, etc.). It is a good idea to keep the instrument cases handy, too, because many parents are concerned about fitting the instrument and its case on the bus or in their cars. Provide adequate space for parents to browse around the instrument table.

Some colorful band posters on the walls and band music playing as people arrive will add to the excitement of the evening. I have a table set aside where I place all brochures and flyers that I receive from the local music stores; parents may help themselves to them. If you will need a microphone, have this set up and tested in advance.

THE MEETING

Parents appreciate a brief and well-organized meeting—many will have left children at home and will be eager to get back after working all day. The meeting should last no more than an hour. The following format works well.

Introduce Yourself

A brief sentence or two is sufficient: "Good evening. I'm Mrs. Fraedrich, the band director here at Cherry Run. Thank you for coming tonight to our band informational meeting. I'm excited to see such enthusiasm for band among our students and parents."

State your agenda for the meeting:
- First I would like to tell you briefly about our band program.
- Then we will hear some instrument demonstrations.
- Then I will talk a little more about the band program and about how to obtain an instrument.
- Finally, I will answer questions.

Briefly talk about the band program:
- Size and activities of this school band
- Place of band in this school's curriculum
- Eligibility
- Cost
- Necessary background
- Scheduling
- Rental of instruments

I make this a brief overview so that the student demonstrators will not have to sit through the entire meeting. After their demonstrations, I can elaborate on some of the topics mentioned here.

Demonstrate Instruments

Handle this in the same way that you did the school recruitment program. I use student demonstrators—usually a different group from the one that performed for the recruitment. Students love to be asked to demonstrate, and this involves more students in the program. Parents enjoy hearing the children perform, and from this they gain an idea of what to expect from their own children after a year's study. Many parents have no experience with band instruments and they enjoy hearing the same "fun facts" that were shared at the children's recruitment program. I use this opportunity to inform the parents about the current popularity of, and demand for, various instruments, and this helps to regulate instrumentation.

This is a good opportunity to elaborate on other aspects of the program which weren't mentioned earlier. Some topics which you may wish to discuss are as follows:

Discuss The Program In Greater Detail

- Extracurricular band opportunities at the elementary level such as area band, solo festival, and private lessons
- The importance of music in a well-rounded education
- Your process for grouping and scheduling classes
- Band opportunities in junior high and high school such as marching band, jazz band, travel, district band, and all-state band
- College—the importance of fine arts activities for admission and the scholarship opportunities for instrumentalists

Prior to the parent meeting, contact local music stores for their instrument rental rates and policies. Most stores have some literature which they will send you. Familiarize yourself with the plans offered by your local stores. Payment periods will probably be monthly, quarterly, or yearly, depending on the policy of the store. In general, the longer the period, the lower the average monthly cost.

Discuss Acquisition Of Instruments

I recommend that parents ask the dealer the following questions:
- Is the monthly rental fee applied toward the purchase price of the instrument? (Am I renting to own?)
- If I rent a used instrument now, can that rental money be applied toward the purchase of a new instrument later?
- Are repairs covered?
- If the instrument needs to be sent out for repair, do you provide loaner instruments?

Most schools have some instruments available for student rental. Often these are the larger instruments such as the tuba, baritone, French horn, tenor saxophone, or bass clarinet which are unavailable or extremely expensive to rent privately. The relatively low rental fees and the convenience of getting the instrument through the school often appeal to people. Know your own inventory and the current school rental prices.

You will have an idea of your instrumentation before this meeting because forms will have been turned in. If you know that you will have too few baritones to go around, have some plan for determining who will get a school instrument and who will not, assuming that everyone will want one. Financial need may be a consideration. Often the principal can advise you in this regard. In cases where all else seems equal, drawing names may be the best method. If this selection process results in a student's having to rent privately, know where that instrument can be rented if it is not available in the local shops. It would be a shame to lose a potential low brass player (always in demand) for want of the instrument.

In some school systems it is possible to borrow instruments from other schools. I start calling other directors as soon as students begin turning in registration forms to ask if they have any extra instruments. Your school system may have a special form to be completed for inter-school loans.

Some students may have an instrument at home which was played by a sibling, parent, relative or friend. Used instruments are fine to use as long as they are in good working condition. I suggest that parents have the instrument checked over by an instrument technician or bring it in for me to inspect before the start of band. A beginning student who is handicapped by a defective instrument will quickly become frustrated and lose interest.

Many school systems provide for students who are financially needy. In Fairfax County, for example, students who qualify receive free or reduced lunches as well as instruments. Information on aid recipients is usually confidential. You may wish to announce this option at the parents' meeting, and any who qualify can notify you privately.

Discuss Equipment Needs

Parents should be given a list of required equipment and accessories for their child's instrument. (See sample required equipment list—Appendix C.) It is a good idea to display these accessories with the instrument. You may be able to make arrangements for borrowing equipment from your local music store. If you will be requiring a piece of equipment which may not be readily available at the local music store (for example, a plastic oboe reed), it is wise to contact the store in advance. Some stores will add that item to their inventory if they know that you will be requiring it. If not, you will at least be able to save parents the frustration of a wasted trip.

Answer Questions

The following are some commonly asked questions which you should be prepared to answer:

- What if my child wants to quit in the middle of the year?
- What subject will you pull my child out of?
- Do braces pose any problem?
- Will asthma affect my child's ability to play any instrument?
- Is practice required?
- How much practice time is required each day?
- Do band instruments come in different sizes?

SUMMARY

The band parents' informational meeting is the forum for introducing yourself and your band program to the parents, for sharing detailed information regarding acquisition of instruments and accessories, and for addressing any concerns which the parents may have. Remember that all parents want what is best for their children; this is your chance to convey to them that you and your band program will be a positive influence in the lives of their children. ■

A Comparison Of Band Method Books

Selecting an elementary band method book is an important task for the band director. Beginning band students spend most of their practice time working out of a method book. The director who is saddled with a poor or mediocre method book fights an uphill battle; valuable time and energy are spent trying to make up for the book's deficiencies. Before investing what can amount to a sizable sum of money, the director should thoroughly examine available method books and consult with other elementary directors. This chapter can facilitate that process.

In this chapter I compare and contrast several of the more popular band method books. I examine the books in terms of content and presentation. The following first-year method books are reviewed: *Band Today* by James Ployhar, *First Division Band Method* by Fred Weber, *Best in Class* by Bruce Pearson, *Yamaha Band Student* by Sandy Feldstein and John O'Reilly, *Belwin Comprehensive Band Method* by Frank Erickson, *Band Plus* by James Swearingen and Barbara Buehlman, *Essential Elements* by Tom C. Rhodes, Donald Bierschenk and Tim Lautzenheiser, *Learning Unlimited* by Art C. Jenson, *Sounds Spectacular Band Course* by Andrew Balent, *Ed Sueta Band Method* by Ed Sueta, *Standard of Excellence* by Bruce Pearson, *Accent on Achievement* by John O'Reilly and Mark Williams, and *21st Century Band Method* by Jack Bullock and Anthony Maiello.

BAND TODAY, BOOK 1

By James Ployhar, Belwin, 1977.

I have used this book for years; it works well with my students.

■ Content

The book contains three pages of useful introductory information on music theory, holding the instrument, and producing the first tones. A fingering chart and a glossary of musical terms and symbols appear at the end. The book moves at a good pace for beginners, starting with whole notes, covering half notes on the second page, and quarter notes on the third. Once students learn six notes, they work through several pages to perfect them before moving ahead. Several duets and two full-band arrangements are included, providing material for concerts.

I see only a few problems with this book. Like all method books designed to be compatible for mixed instrument classes, the French horn book is in a bad range—notes are either too low or too high for most beginners. Treatment of the clarinet crossing the break (the sometimes difficult to master transition from low to high register) could be better—only a few exercises cover the clarinet high register, and these are thrown in without enough preparatory exercises in this area. I suggest supplementing the clarinet book with your own exercises.

■ Presentation

The book uses a format which appeals to children. The cover is glossy, colorful and interesting. Material is well-spaced on the pages. New information is presented and discussed in boxes directly above where it occurs in the music. A silhouette of a hand points to new notes and ideas, preventing confusion among beginning students. Many of the exercises have titles, making them actual "songs" in the eyes of students. The titles are popular with students: "Really Movin'" (a two-note song which students can play on their first day of band), "Half Note Shuffle," and "Hurrah! A Melody" are a few examples. Many familiar folk songs are included as well.

Occasional "pencil pusher" theory exercises are included (if the book is to be used for more than one year, writing in the books might be a problem). New notes are introduced off to the side along with the corresponding fingering. Some of the newer method books liven up the page by adding a second ink color; this book uses only black ink. The format is clear, uncluttered, and inviting.

FIRST DIVISION BAND METHOD, BOOK I

By Fred Weber, Belwin, 1962.

As you can see from the copyright date, this is an older book, and that is its primary drawback.

■ Content

This book is much like the *Band Today* method in terms of content. Like the *Band Today* book, it includes a fingering chart, an introductory page of music theory, a glossary of musical symbols and terms, and a photograph of playing position. Whole notes are introduced first, followed by quarter notes, and then half notes. New notes are introduced at about the same time and in the same order as in the *Band Today* book. Some written theory exercises are included at points throughout the book. Several duets and two full-band arrangements are provided.

Some of the musical selections are no longer familiar to children— "The Blue Tail Fly," "Red River Valley," and "I'm Called Little Buttercup." Again, the French horn books are in a bad range for the beginner, and little material guides clarinet students crossing the break. Eighth notes are introduced too close to the end of the book with only a few pages after that to perfect this rhythm.

■ Presentation

What was modern in 1962 is now out of date. The two-tone design of the book cover lacks appeal to today's children, although the content is still usable. The pages are nicely designed and appealingly clean and uncluttered. New material is presented in circles above the exercises, and arrows point to the symbol or note being discussed. Titles, such as "Who's the Champ?", head many exercises, even the simplest whole note exercises, and children enjoy this. Introductory photographs of playing position from 1962 look dated today.

The *First Division* book is usable if you already own a set at your school, but if purchasing new books, I recommend a more recent publication with more child-appeal.

BEST IN CLASS, BOOK 1

By Bruce Pearson, Kjos, 1982.

This method book offers some interesting alternatives which band directors may find useful.

■ Content

This is one book that attempts to solve the problem of having to be suitable for a class of mixed instruments while also addressing the specific problems of the individual instruments. The notes that are easiest for beginning flutists are different from those easiest for beginning trumpeters—each instrument is unique in this regard. When grouping classes heterogeneously in terms of instrumentation, a compromise must occur if one method book is to be used. To have most instruments begin on acceptable notes (not too high, not too low, not too difficult to finger, etc.) some instruments must compromise a great deal—i.e., French horns are in a bad range, flutes must use difficult fingerings, trumpet notes are a little high for some students. The *Best in Class* method solves this problem by including supplemental yellow pages. These pages occurring throughout the book utilize the "best" starting notes and range for each instrument. The book is effectively two books in one. For example, each page of the French horn book is transposed to a better key on the yellow pages. While these are not compatible for playing simultaneously with other instruments, they allow the French horn students to experience success on their own rather than having them strain with frustration for notes that are too high or too low.

The book moves faster and covers more material than most beginning books. The last pages of this book correspond to the beginning and middle sections of volume two in most methods. Although the book is the same length as other books, more is crowded onto one page. Eighth notes appear less than halfway through the book. The clarinets must deal with the high register earlier than in most books; they are provided with many exercises for perfecting this, but the exercises are rather difficult.

This book recognizes and attempts to solve many of the problems encountered by band directors. I like it very much for older beginners and for elementary students who might have band more than once a week. It moves a little fast for the forty-five minute, once-a-week students.

■ Presentation

The book cover is appealing to children with its colorful collage of instrument photographs. Unlike the previous books, this book introduces additional colors on the pages—red, blue, yellow and gray—making an attractive presentation.

New material is boxed in red in a prominent spot on the page. This feature is set off by a red head/light bulb which appears in the margin whenever there is a new idea. A blue eighth note appears in the margin when there is a new note, a yellow star for special exercises (the other books call these "bonus lines") and a gray pencil for written theory exercises. My students never seemed to catch on to the color coding system, but appreciated the splash of color on the page. All tunes are numbered consecutively (the book goes up to number 149) and are given titles—most other books begin each page with number one.

My only criticism regarding appearance is that the book looks cluttered. Staves and notes are in smaller print than the other books, and more material is squeezed onto a page. Bright elementary students or older students might enjoy the stimulation; many of mine found it to be too busy and intimidating.

YAMAHA BAND STUDENT, BOOK I

By Sandy Feldstein and John O'Reilly, Alfred, 1988.

(Accompaniment C.D. or cassette tape available.) This is an excellent, up-to-date method book.

■ Content

As do the other method books discussed, this book includes a fingering chart. No glossary or introductory notes are included. Children enjoy the full-page "certificate of achievement" included at the end of the book.

Early exercises are not titled, merely numbered. Familiar folk tunes have titles, however. Several full-band arrangements appear throughout the book, not merely at the end, as with the other books. The book includes many familiar songs.

The *Yamaha Band Student* moves quickly, reaching eighth notes very early, and reaching dotted quarter notes (which don't even occur in book one of the *First Division* or *Band Today* books) about halfway through the book.

The treatment of crossing the clarinet break is one of the smoothest of the books reviewed. It begins with the easier notes above the break and works down toward the B (the break) and C which are always the most difficult notes for clarinetists. All of the other books introduce the break using the notes B and C, making the crossing unnecessarily difficult for students.

This method book contains all of the information provided by the other method books, and more. It presents the information in a clear, appealing format. Lengthy theory explanations are left to the teacher, reducing the clutter on the page, but perhaps making this book a little more difficult for students to use in moving ahead on their own.

■ Presentation

The book cover appeals to students of all ages with its glossy, colorful photograph of their particular instruments. Pages are nicely spaced, and staves and notes are a good size for beginners. All titles and etude numbers appear in red, and new material is presented at the top of each page in a pink shaded area with white boxes and black lettering. This format is appealing and organized. It is matter-of-fact and clear—equally suitable for children or for older beginners.

BELWIN COMPREHENSIVE BAND METHOD, BOOK 1
By Frank Erickson, Belwin, 1989.

This method is designed to be equally effective when used with either a heterogeneous or homogeneous instrument grouping.

■ Content

As do some of the other books discussed, this method book includes a fingering chart, a written introduction to playing the instrument and an introductory note-reading/music theory page. In addition, it includes a blank page of staff paper which could come in handy. Seven full-band arrangements are included.

The book is divided into two sections which can be used for like instrument classes or for a mixed band class. The notes selected for the mixed instrument class are those in the easiest playing range for beginners; however, the trade-off is that some students play harmony parts, in order to remain in the best range, rather than the entire class playing a unison melody part. This could create further problems: children usually want to play the melody, but only some will be able to, and French horn players and other brass beginners, struggling to find their pitches, may have a more difficult time when the class is not playing in unison. The advantages outweigh the difficulties, however, and I feel that this book has a great deal of merit.

■ Presentation

The book is attractive. The pages are uncluttered and easy to read. New information is presented in gray boxes for a clear and concise presentation. The book cover is not the glossy, photo cover of some of the methods, but it is serviceable.

BAND PLUS, BOOK I

By James Swearingen and Barbara Buehlman, Heritage, 1984 and 1989.

The strength of this book is its interesting and appealing musical games and puzzles.

■ Content

As do most of the other methods, this book includes introductory pages discussing instrument assembly and care, tone production, playing position and the basics of music. Also included are a fingering chart, a blank staff paper page, a glossary, an assignment sheet and a practice record.

No attempt has been made to overcome the incompatibility, in terms of beginning range, of heterogeneous instrument groupings. Consequently, the French horn must play either very high or very low to match the pitches of the other instruments. The starting pitches of many instruments are a compromise—not the best notes, but not too bad, either. Many of the new method books do address the incompatibility problem, but most of the older books do not.

The treatment of the clarinet crossing the break is a little fast, without enough preparatory exercises. Several full-band arrangements are included, and all books contain both melody and harmony parts. Everyone gets a chance to play the melody (important to children), but the director can assign players to harmony parts to customize the arrangement for a particular group of students.

■ Presentation

The book is appealing to children with its fun puzzles and games, its cartoon-like illustrations of some new material and its use of fun titles for almost every exercise. New material is presented in boxes. One negative feature is the crowded, busy appearance of the pages: this clutter can be a distraction to some students.

ESSENTIAL ELEMENTS, BOOK I

By Tom C. Rhodes, Donald Bierschenk and Tim Lautzenheiser, Hal Leonard, 1991. (Accompaniment C.D. or cassette tape available.)

This is one of several new methods available offering the option of using pre-recorded accompaniments. This book seems to be well-planned and includes the best aspects of a variety of different method books.

■ Content

The standard introductory notes on tone production and instrument assembly are included, as are a fingering chart and glossary. A nice added feature is the historical information presented throughout the book. A brief history of that particular instrument is included at the beginning of the student books. Many subsequent pages contain historical paragraphs about composers or musical events. Concepts such as tuning are discussed—most beginning method books do not address the topic of tuning. The book contains some duets as well as some full-band arrangements.

* National Standards Supplement

The problem of making the book equally suitable for use in mixed instrument classes as well as homogeneous groupings is dealt with in two ways: supplementary pages, in purple, are included for use with the homogeneous grouping—these pages keep the instrument in its best starting range, but are not compatible, pitch-wise, with the books of different instruments. The white pages are for use with mixed instruments; in order to eliminate the problem of putting some instruments in a bad range to make them compatible, the notes on these pages are not in unison. French horns, for example, have harmony notes which allow them to stay in a good starting range while playing along with the rest of the band. The one difficulty may be that of finding pitches on the French horn.

The treatment of the clarinet crossing the break seems to be one of the better approaches. It is introduced gradually, and several stepwise exercises are included to help clarinets with this often difficult technique.

■ **Presentation**

The bright, colorful cover is appealing to elementary children. The use of purple ink to set off new material in the book is a nice idea. Purple supplemental pages contrast well with standard white pages, making it easy to distinguish between these two sections. The pages are a bit busier than some other method books discussed here, but it would not deter me from using this book.

SOUNDS SPECTACULAR BAND COURSE, BOOK 1

By Andrew Balent, Carl Fischer, 1991.

This is another new book with some nice features.

■ **Content**

This method is similar to many of the newer methods in terms of content. Some added features are three written quizzes, a practice record, a section for ensemble fun, a page of pieces with piano accompaniment and two band arrangements. The ensembles include all parts in each book.

The book attempts to solve the problem of having some instruments playing in poor ranges in order to be compatible with others in a mixed instrument grouping. Its solution is the same as that of some of the other books mentioned here—not all instruments are in unison at the beginning of the book. This allows the French horn, for example, to remain in a good starting register while playing harmony parts; however, after the first few pages, the French horn moves upward quickly.

A good feature of the percussion books is the inclusion of bell parts for every exercise (often directors must order separate bell and percussion books.)

One band arrangement in book one, *Old MacDonald*, coordinates with an arrangement in book two, *Old Mac Rocks*. The two can be performed together on a concert if the director wishes to combine beginners with advanced students.

■ **Presentation**

The book is easy to read with clean, uncluttered pages. The use of red stars to set off new material is good. It is a well-organized presentation.

ED SUETA BAND METHOD, BOOK I

By Ed Sueta, Macie Publishing Co., 1974. (Accompaniment tape available.)

Ed Sueta's strong focus on rhythm is a noteworthy characteristic of this book.

■ Content

This book is different from many others in a few respects. There is less written information provided in the book—for students who wish to go ahead on their own, this can be a problem; however, more musical exercises are then included on each page. Consequently, book one will take students farther than some of the other methods' first books.

A section of twelve "rhythm vocabulary charts" is included at the end of the book for clapping and counting practice. These exercises coordinate with the various lessons. Emphasis is placed on coordination between the foot (tapping) and fingers (playing).

Supplementary pages are included to deal with problem areas—i.e., the clarinet crossing the break and the French horn range problem. The French horns can begin on supplementary lessons A-L which are in a good range. The pages which are compatible with the rest of the band start later and put the horn in a worse range. The clarinet book includes a supplementary section on crossing the break. The exercises are good, and there are many of them; however, the clarinet book gets difficult quickly after the introduction to crossing the break.

■ Presentation

This book does not have much child-appeal. Its plain beige cover and its unadorned pages are rather dull looking; however, the pages are well-spaced and easy to read. There are few titled songs at the beginning of the book—just numbered exercises; most elementary children seem to prefer songs with titles. Familiar tunes are included as the book progresses.

The supplementary pages are white, as are the standard pages, and this may be confusing to students. Using a contrasting color for supplementary pages, as some of the other method books do, would make this book easier to use. There are two sets of pages with the same page numbers—one in the supplementary section and one in the band section—and this duplication of page numbers might add to confusion.

STANDARD OF EXCELLENCE, BOOK I

By Bruce Pearson, Kjos, 1993. (Accompaniment C.D. or cassette tape available.)

This is a method book that is designed to be equally useful in classes of one instrument, with one section of the band or with the full band.

■ Content

This method book combines many of the best features of the other methods discussed. It includes color drawings of playing position, instrument assembly and instrument care. Also included are a glossary, fingering chart, practice card, history of the instrument, a scale page and rhythm studies.

Optional starting pages are included for many instruments for use in a class of like instruments. Other pages can be used for a mixed instrument grouping within the section (woodwind, brass) or for full band. Optional notes are given for certain instruments, to ensure that the instrument remains in an acceptable beginning range in any class grouping

The book has a few full-band arrangements. Exercises termed "Excellerators" are fun for students who go ahead on their own or need a challenge. Many familiar songs are included.

■ Presentation

The pages are well-spaced and easy to read. New material is presented in yellow boxes with red stripes. The format is appealing and well-organized. Most exercises are titled, which children enjoy.

LEARNING UNLIMITED—CLASS SERIES, BOOK I

By Art C. Jenson, Hal Leonard, 1973. (Accompaniment cassette tape available.)

This was one of the first popular method books to include accompaniment tapes.

■ Content

This band method has a supplementary book called the "Learning Unlimited Individualized Band Series (LUBS)." Without the supplement, the book does not seem to offer as much material as many of the other methods. With the supplement, the method becomes more expensive than what many directors are willing or able to buy.

The problem of making the method book suitable for each individual instrument as well as for a mixed instrument class is not dealt with; consequently, some instruments are in a bad range from the beginning.

Some of the positive features of this method book are the puzzles, the duets and ensembles, and the concert pieces.

■ Presentation

This book has a different approach than most to teaching the first lesson. Note reading is not introduced immediately, as it is in most methods. Instead, letter names are written inside black lines representing the length of the notes. Children learn to finger and blow the first notes and to play some simple tunes before note reading is introduced.

The use of orange ink, in addition to the standard black, creates a nice contrast and highlights new material. The pages are a bit crowded and busy—some students can be overwhelmed and confused by too much material on a page. There is a coordination chart included that tells what LUBS exercise coordinates with the student's level in the method book—it may be confusing to some elementary students.

ACCENT ON ACHIEVEMENT, BOOK I

By John O'Reilly and Mark Williams, Alfred, 1997. (Accompaniment C.D. or cassette tape available.)

This method book has many excellent features.

■ Content

Like many of the method books, this book has introductory pages covering instrument assembly and care, playing position, embouchure formation, tone production, music theory background, a glossary, fingering chart and practice chart, as well as scale pages, rhythm pages, and special supplementary pages. Optional starting pages are included for French horn and oboe.

Choice of music is one of the best features of this book. There are many familiar tunes, as well as tunes from nineteen different countries and twenty-two classical composers. There are five full-band arrangements and a variety of solos, duets and rounds.

✳ National Standard Supplement

Some fun written exercises are included—students can compose, improvise or choose an orchestration for a song. If the book is to be used for several years, writing in it may be a problem; however, the ideas are good.

■ Presentation

The book's presentation is one of its strongest points. It is well-organized—

new material is presented in colorful boxes on the page tops and high-lighted on the pages. It is very appealing visually with its glossy, multicolor cover and colorful drawings which accompany many exercises. Every exercise is titled and numbered. Children would enjoy this presentation.

21ST CENTURY BAND METHOD, BOOK 1

By Jack Bullock and Anthony Maiello, Warner Brothers/Belwin, 1996. (Accompaniment C.D., play-along video and Vivace® Intelligent Accompanist.™)

■ Content

This method book is very progressive in its incorporation of both video and Vivace® accompaniment. It would be an excellent method for middle school beginning bands which might have Vivace® and be able to utilize fully that exciting component of the book—I'm not sure how many elementary bands have such a budget. However, the book is excellent on its own.

Unlike many of the methods discussed, student books in this series do not include introductory pages covering instrument assembly and care, tone production or embouchure formation—this information is presented in the accompanying video. A practice chart, fingering chart and music theory page are included.

Students will recognize many familiar tunes throughout the book. Several pieces are included for concerts. There are pieces from many different countries.

The book begins with the standard starting pitches, concert D, Eb and F. Eighth notes are introduced in lesson five, which is earlier than in most methods. Treatment of the clarinet crossing the break seems fairly good. The French horn book contains optional alternate starting pages, allowing the beginning horn student to start in a good range. Drums and mallets are taught in two separate books—some methods combine the two.

Student books contain very little written information such as theory or historical background, relying on the video to present this material. Students might have difficulty going ahead on their own without the video or teacher.

■ Presentation

The book is attractively presented. While not as colorful as some of the other methods discussed (this method uses two ink colors—black and blue), pages are well-planned, with new material presented in blue boxes. Each tune is numbered and titled, which students enjoy. With limited written information in the student books, there is even more room for musical exercises, without a cluttered look. ■

Scheduling And Grouping Of Classes

The scheduling and grouping of classes requires creativity and flexibility on the part of the elementary school band director. Having a supportive and cooperative school administration and staff is a tremendous asset when scheduling; without school support, the band director is often forced to compromise program ideals and consequently feels resentful. Each school system sets its own guidelines for instrumental music. In most school systems that offer elementary band, it is a pull-out program—students are pulled out of the regular classroom during the school day; therefore, the band schedule must be coordinated around the school schedule. This is easier said than done. With so many other specialty programs vying for the same students' time—speech, physical education, resource, gifted and talented, physical therapy, guidance, chorus, student council association—coordinating schedules can be difficult. The following approach has worked well for me.

BEGINNING CLASSES

I teach the following beginning classes: flute, oboe, clarinet, saxophone, trumpet, French horn, trombone, baritone, tuba, and percussion. A grouping popular among band directors (and the one that I favor) is the grouping of beginners homogeneously by instrument. This enables me to maximize the class time since instruction focuses completely on one instrument. The Music Program of Studies (POS) for the Fairfax County Public School system recommends the homogeneous grouping for beginners; however, many teachers have to travel to several schools during the week and lack the time at one school to offer a separate class for each instrument. The POS then suggests, as one possibility, the grouping of clarinets with saxophones, and trombones with baritones and tubas. If further consolidation is needed, the POS suggests combining the French horns in with another class. I do not recommend this. The difficulty of the instrument and its incompatibility with other instruments in terms of comfortable starting range necessitate a separate class.

Classroom teachers are sometimes opposed to the homogenous grouping since it means more interruptions to their teaching day. A teacher with only one beginner on each instrument already has ten interruptions where students are leaving the classroom. Compromise may be necessary if the director is to maintain the integrity of his program while maintaining a positive and cooperative relationship with the classroom teachers. One idea might be to group the students homogeneously during the first half of the year when students are learning the specifics of their instruments such as fingerings and sound production. During the second half of the year, the director can occasionally or frequently take students in homeroom groupings of mixed instruments. This has advantages for everyone. The students love being with their classmates and hearing how all of the instruments sound when mixed together—they enjoy having their own mini-band. The size of the group is manageable for the director and can even facilitate fitting together the various instrumental parts in a piece of sheet music prior to a full band rehearsal. With spring concerts right around the corner, this is a benefit. A homeroom grouping of students also means fewer classes overall for the band teacher. The additional time allows the director to plan for concerts, type programs, help students with music for solo festivals, prepare spring instrument rental contracts, and complete enrollment reports and other required paperwork. Flexibility and communication with classroom teachers are the keys to successful scheduling.

ADVANCED CLASSES

After students have established a solid musical foundation in their first year, it is often desirable to regroup in a student's second year of band. A standard grouping, time permitting, would have advanced students divided into three groups: advanced woodwinds, advanced brass, and advanced percussion. I use this approach with my advanced students, and it works well for them. Occasionally I may regroup to work more in-depth with one section. Once a month I combine all three advanced classes; students enjoy and benefit from the full band experience. This mixed grouping works at the advanced level where students have already mastered many of the important concepts of their specific instruments. I would not recommend this grouping for beginners.

Faced with complaints of fragmentation by classroom teachers and with parental concerns over children missing instructional time in the classroom, many elementary band directors have tried alternative approaches to scheduling. Two such alternative approaches are the rotating schedule and the team teaching approach.

ALTERNATIVE APPROACHES

The advantage of the rotating schedule is that it prevents students from being pulled out of the same subject each week. In a typical day, a director might teach seven forty-five-minute classes which we will call periods one through seven. In week one, students are assigned to a certain period. In week two, all students are shifted down to the next time period. Students that meet during seventh period in week one will meet during first period in week two (then second period in week three, etc.). A possible disadvantage to this scheduling concept is the confusion of the students as to what time they should report to band. Band directors who have successfully employed this approach insist that after the first few weeks no one has trouble with the rotation. Even if students do forget their times, they are in school with their instruments on the correct day, and the director can always send for them. Rotating the scheduled <u>day</u> for band would not be advisable because problems might arise with students forgetting which day they should bring their instruments to school.

Rotating Schedule

The team teaching concept, where two or more directors "service" one school in a fraction of the time that it would take one director, is a popular approach and has been tried in some Fairfax County schools. Team teaching reduces fragmentation for the classroom teacher: if all band teachers coordinate schedules and teach classes at the same times, the result is a smaller number of interruptions of the classroom teacher's day. The classroom teacher can plan around this time block. Most classroom teachers find this preferable to having small groups of students coming and going all day long. Team teaching offers several benefits to band directors as well as to classroom teachers. The opportunity to exchange ideas and to share information with musical colleagues is one such benefit. Just having

Team Teaching

someone to commiserate or rejoice with over the students' progress is a treat for the often-isolated band director. The capability of one director to cover the other director's classes in an absence is a further advantage. Since substitutes are often not available for itinerant teachers, students would otherwise miss their weekly lesson.

If team teaching is to be successful, however, a few conditions must be met. First, there must be adequate space in the building for multiple teachers to teach simultaneously. Many elementary schools are overcrowded; one utility room serves as work space for all itinerant teachers who are in the building on their different days. Unless all teachers have an acceptable teaching space, the team-teaching approach cannot work.

Second, there must be sufficient equipment for two or more teachers to use simultaneously. Extra music stands, for example, may need to be purchased to outfit all classes. Third, the team teachers must have a joint planning time in order to coordinate their efforts. Otherwise the result will be several distinct bands rather than one unified group. Lastly, the teachers must be flexible in their approaches and open to new ideas. Occasional compromises may be necessary, and the directors must make the effort to work cooperatively. ∎

The Well-Constructed Lesson

The average elementary band teacher may teach as many as forty lessons each week. Careful planning is required to ensure that each of these lessons is the best that it can be. One or two mediocre lessons out of forty may seem insignificant, but for the students in those classes, who receive only a few minutes of instruction each week, the impact can be significant. A good lesson should include the following:

- The lesson has been planned; goals have been set.
- Chairs and music stands are set up for class.
- Supplementary exercises, sheet music, and materials to be handed out are ready—perhaps on the chairs as the students enter.
- Everything that can be done ahead of time to maximize the time spent on actual instruction has been done.

PREPARATION

I always place a pencil on each stand and a blank practice card on each chair before students arrive. If I will be passing out letters or sheet music, I place these on their chairs also. I often go through their sheet music before passing it out to mark or circle potential problem spots. This saves a great deal of time in class. (Asking a class of elementary students to mark something on their music often results in confusion and wasted time; however, there are times when students may learn more by marking it themselves. The director must decide.)

WARM-UP (5–10 Minutes) | The warm-up is sometimes considered to be the most important part of the lesson; it should not be overlooked. It is as important to the musician as stretching exercises are to an athlete. In addition to physically preparing the student to play the instrument, the warm-up helps to mentally prepare the students for class by focusing their attention and energy. Students may unpack and begin warming up on their own as they wait for the rest of the class to arrive. This is a good time for the teacher to greet and talk to various students. Once everyone has arrived, the warm-up should begin.

Brass | A warm-up is particularly important for beginning brass players who are just developing the muscles which form the embouchure. Beginning with a pitch matching exercise and advancing to an interval exercise works well. I have students, in a group and individually, match my pitch on various notes. Make a game of it as different students play the pitches in response. This process assumes that the teacher has access to, and is able to play, the instrument. Resourceful teachers can usually come up with demonstrator instruments, and all band teachers should be able to play these instruments—if not, practice or take some lessons to improve competency. (Modelling of the instrument is extremely important.) In about thirty seconds you can hear each student individually and can easily identify and correct many problems—i.e., a student may not tongue, may not support the air, or may be puffing the cheeks.

The interval study in Figure 1 is excellent for developing the lip and the ear. I find this exercise so useful because it gets students thinking in terms of "low," "medium," and "high" buzzes for each fingering. Beginners may not always be able to produce the highest or lowest notes, but this will come as their lip muscles develop. Beginning brass players are confronted with the problem of being able to produce more than one pitch from a fingering—how do they know which is the correct pitch? Let's say that they want to play an open "G," but they are not sure if they are getting the G or a C (which is also an open fingering). Once they realize that the G uses a medium buzz, they can play their interval exercise and pick out the medium-buzz pitch—G. After a few weeks, their lips will be accustomed to the feel of a G and this process will not be necessary, but it is an excellent method for beginning students to find their starting pitches when practicing at home where a teacher is not around to say "You're starting too high or too low."

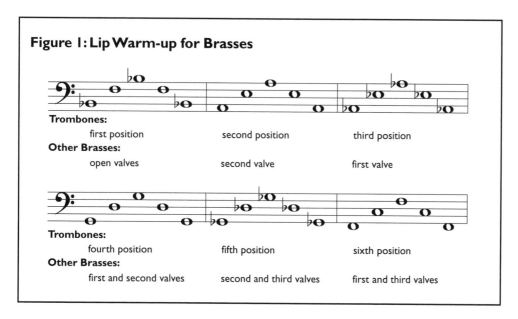

Figure 1: Lip Warm-up for Brasses

Trombones:
    first position   second position   third position
Other Brasses:
    open valves   second valve   first valve

Trombones:
    fourth position   fifth position   sixth position
Other Brasses:
    first and second valves   second and third valves   first and third valves

I have my students copy down the fingering progression: 0, 2, 1, 1 & 2, 2 & 3, 1 & 3 in their books, and I tell them to begin their practice at home by playing low, medium, and high buzzes on each fingering. (Corresponding trombone positions for the exercise are 1, 2, 3, 4, 5, 6.)

Woodwinds

The same interval warm-ups can be used for woodwinds, but unlike the brasses, woodwinds will need to change fingerings for each note. I generally prefer a simpler warm-up for them: a scale, a breathing exercise (maybe a contest to see who can hold a note the longest), or a note review.

Percussion

Having a weekly warm-up routine is a good idea. This may include some stretching exercises, to limber up shoulders, arms and wrists, as well as some rudimentary exercises. The following is a suggested routine:

- Right hand single strokes
- Left hand single strokes
- Alternating hands—single strokes
- Right hand double bounces
- Left hand double bounces
- Alternating hands—double bounces
- Gradually speed up the above
- Long roll

While students are playing, the teacher should be observing and offering reminders on factors such as hand position, stick height, or arm movement.

REVIEW (15 minutes)

Review is an essential part of a successful lesson; previously learned material will provide a foundation for the new concepts to be covered this week. It is easy for students who meet only once a week to forget what they learned in the previous lesson—this is especially true if the students have not practiced as instructed during the week.

For the first few months, my review includes a flash card game. I keep a folder for each class with flash cards of the notes that they have learned. When I hold up the card, they name the note and then play it. We do this as a group and individually. With the first few cards of the day, I'll ask the students to give me a saying for the lines or spaces and then use that saying to determine the name of the note.

After the note review, I generally select exercises from the previous weeks' lessons to further review. In addition to having students perform the exercises, it is important to verbally go over the concepts that were learned previously to ensure understanding. Students enjoy playing these tunes that they have already perfected, and the class begins with the students feeling successful.

Review is a process that continues throughout the lesson. Even when covering new concepts, the teacher should be constantly reminding students of previously learned concepts, showing how they tie in to each other. For example, an exercise that focuses on dynamic contrasts can also provide material to review articulation and rhythm and note reading. All of these factors combine to produce a unique musical product.

NEW MATERIAL (20 Minutes)

The review should easily carry over into the introduction of new material. Generally, the band method book is the basic tool for teaching new concepts. If a new note is coming up in an exercise, relate the new fingering to a fingering that students already know (i.e., "The new note for flutes is A flat. Finger a G; now add your left pinky to that"). Try to make an easy transition between the old and the new. Having students name the notes and finger through an exercise before attempting to play it can smooth the transition and facilitate success while minimizing frustration.

Don't be restricted by the method book—I pick and choose the exercises that I feel will work best with a particular class. I may skip around in the book to cover new material in a different sequence if I feel that this would work best. Even the best method books need occasional supplementing when used with certain classes. When teaching the clarinet high register/crossing the break, for example, I often write out additional exercises since most method books cover this topic quickly.

Each class of students is different, and the teacher can tailor-make exercises for that class if necessary. Of course, creating and writing out musical exercises can be time consuming; once done, they should be filed away for future use. If the teacher must frequently supplement the book in this manner, then it may be wise to study and select a different method book (see the Comparison of Band Method Books, chapter three). Other sources of supplementary material include sheet music, supplementary technique books, and music theory workbooks. Many method books are published as part of a series that includes these companion books and sheet music. These supplementary materials are then correlated with the method book and are designed to reinforce particular concepts.

When covering new material, it is important to have the students try it during class to ensure that they understand the concept before leaving. Allow sufficient time during class for practice of the new material. If time is running short and there may not be enough time to do more than verbally cover new concepts, it is probably best to wait and introduce the material at the next lesson rather than risk ending the class with children feeling confused and hurried.

ASSIGNMENT AND SUMMARY (5 Minutes)

The transition from "New Material" to "Assignment" is naturally smooth since the assignment should be drawn mainly from the exercises that were discussed in class. If a special supplementary page or book is to be used, take the time to go over this. Allow time for students to ask questions about the assignment.

It is useful to end the class by summing up what has been covered in this lesson. Students may provide the summation themselves by answering the question, "What did we learn today?" If the lesson plan was outlined on the board, the teacher may wish to use this as a summary check list. The summary provides closure to the lesson.

Have students write down their assignment for next week before they leave class. The teacher, too, should be sure to keep a written record of the assignment. This is best recorded in your lesson plan book. When teaching so many classes each week, it is easy to forget who was assigned what. There should be a routine established for the "assignment" portion of the lesson. I give my students weekly practice cards which have a special place for writing the assignment. (See sample practice cards—Appendix D.) I write the assignment on the board and have the students copy this down on their next week's practice cards. (The pencils and practice cards were distributed before class started. The previous week's cards were collected at the beginning of class.)

The following suggestions may help you to plan and carry out a successful lesson:

1. **Use students' names often**—this not only helps you to learn students' names, but studies show that children respond positively to the use of their names.

2. **Maximize playing time**—"doing" is the best way for students to learn. Be efficient with explanations to allow more time for playing. Break up lengthy, difficult explanations with playing in between.

3. **Try to hear each student individually**—even if it's only a note or two. This may be difficult with a large class, but it takes only a minute or two to work around a room and hear each student tongue a note or slur two notes. This helps you to spot problems which may have gone unnoticed, and it gives each student a moment of your undivided attention. This is important to children.

4. **Be generous with encouragement and praise.** The praise should be specific rather than general (i.e., "You fingered those high register notes perfectly!" rather than "You are good!") Sandwich corrections in between positive comments—i.e., "You really blew that note with excellent tone! Now try using your tongue to start the sound. There you go!" I try to find one good thing to say about each student's performance which will make him/her feel special—it may be tone, articulation, posture, fingerings, embouchure, or note reading. Remember that all students like to feel that they stand out at something.

5. **Demonstrate frequently and play along with students.** This is how they form their concept of proper tone and playing technique. A demonstration is worth a thousand words. As a teacher, you should model correct musical habits for your students.

6. **Make learning fun.** Children love games and surprises, and these can be incorporated into the lesson. A note-reading game can be fun for students. (See sample note-reading game—Appendix F). Make up a music trivia game to play while students are packing up or need a break. Bring in an unusual instrument or a recording of a performance on their instrument. Pass out a special song that you know they would enjoy playing. Surprise them with a reward—stickers or pencils—for good work. Challenge them to play a certain exercise perfectly for a prize. Encourage students to write and bring in their own songs—play these in class. Be creative! ∎

Everyday
Instrument Repairs

One aspect of elementary band directing that can be daunting to many directors, but which you can expect to encounter daily, is that of instruments that do not work properly. Many directors feel inadequate in the area of instrument repair—they are trained to play the instruments, but know little about the mechanics involved. For even the most minor repairs, they send the student to the repair shop, which means that the student is without an instrument for at least a week. This gap is unnecessary. A simple understanding of how the instrument operates is all that is needed. If you can take a repair class, it would be beneficial, but if not, merely sitting down with an instrument for a few minutes to examine it can be enlightening. Once you realize that there are only so many things that can go wrong with an instrument, you can begin to troubleshoot. In many cases, a simple adjustment is all that is required. Few directors have the time or equipment to perform lengthy major repairs—those can be sent out to trained instrument repair people.

I recommend having a mouthpiece handy for every instrument that you teach; that way you can easily play the instrument yourself to determine the problem. With beginning students, always consider the possibility of student error—often the student is doing something incorrectly, such as accidentally pushing on a key that should not be pushed, and this results in a squeak or some other unexpected sound.

Always start by checking the most obvious problems first. I have wasted valuable class time playing a problem instrument, checking for leaks and testing the mechanism, only to realize that a broken reed was at fault all along. The table of everyday repair problems and solutions, at the end of this chapter, should aid in handling most band instrument repairs encountered by elementary directors.

BRASSES

Brass instruments are fairly simple to understand, but not always to repair. They all operate on the harmonic (overtone) series which allows many different notes to be played using one fingering. The valves add additional lengths of tubing to the instrument, when they are depressed, and can be used in combination for a variety of tube lengths. In the case of the trombone, the slide lengthens the tubing. Brass instruments can then produce any pitch in the overtone series for any of the lengths of tubing. This capability makes it possible to play a chromatic scale. Understanding this simple valve/tube mechanism is the first step in brass instrument repair.

While most woodwind repairs are simple adjustments, brass repairs often involve body work. Brass instruments require more routine maintenance—oiling valves, greasing slides, cleaning out the tubing—and, consequently, many brass problems are the result of poor maintenance. Other common brass problems are frequently the result of a drop (dents, stuck valves, stuck mouthpiece, broken water key) or user error (valves in incorrectly). Knowing the causes of brass problems can help to alleviate some future problems.

The equipment and time required to do body work on brass instruments make some repairs impractical for the band director—send those repairs to a professional; however, there are many repairs that any band director can handle with a minimum of time and equipment. The most common are described in this chapter.

WOODWINDS

All woodwind instruments share their basic mechanism; if you understand how a flute works, you can apply that knowledge to any other woodwind instrument. The woodwind mechanism is more intricate and complex than that of the brasses. Because rods, springs, levers, and keys work together to control the woodwind instruments' operation, the potential for problems is greater than on a brass instrument with its simple valve and tube system.

While the basic key mechanism is similar on all woodwinds, each wood-wind instrument has some unique characteristics, requiring specific mention by instrument in this table. An entire chapter could be devoted to the oboe; its delicate and intricate mechanism offers the greatest potential for adjustment problems. Oboe repairs, other than the basics mentioned here, should probably be handled by a trained repair person.

Percussion repairs are largely routine maintenance—replacing worn parts and adjusting equipment. Most elementary schools are lucky if they own some percussion equipment—a snare drum, bass drum and cymbals are standard. Percussion repairs are necessary infrequently; however, when a repair is needed, it can pose a major problem unless the director has some idea of what to do. The following table should aid the beginning director in carrying out standard percussion repairs.

▌PERCUSSION

The following tools and accessories should be included in your instrument repair tool box:

▌Recommended Repair Tools

Mouthpiece puller (There are a variety of types. A one-piece model is the most portable for a traveling teacher.)

Valve oil (I recommend Space Filler™ brand nontoxic oil. It is fine for all brass instruments and is the only nontoxic oil that I have been able to find.)

French horn string

Slide grease

Small crochet hook (for reattaching woodwind springs)

Extra clarinet and flute pads

Jewelers screwdrivers

Pad cement

Stick shellac

Small needle-nosed pliers

Rag or handkerchief

Large adjustable pliers for removing stuck valve caps

Masking tape

Vaseline

Assorted rubber bands

Your own mouthpiece for every instrument

Suggested Instrument Repair And Maintenance Books

Hunt, Norman J. *Guide to Teaching Brass*. Dubuque: William C. Brown, 1968.

Mueller, Kenneth A. *Complete Guide to the Maintenance and Repair of Band Instruments*. West Nyack, New York: Parker, 1982.

Schmidt, Robert. *A Clarinetist's Notebook. Vol. I: Care and Repair*, 1971.

Springer, George H. *Maintenance and Repair of Band Instruments for Band Directors and Instrumentalists*. Boston: Allyn and Bacon, 1970.

Stanley, Burton. *Instrument Repair for the Music Teacher*. Sherman Oaks, CA: Alfred, 1978.

Tiede, Clayton H. *Practical Band Instrument Repair Manual*. 3rd ed. Dubuque: William C. Brown, 1976.

Timm, Everett L. *The Woodwinds*. 2nd ed. Boston: Allyn and Bacon, 1971.

Westphal, Frederick W. *Guide to Teaching Woodwinds*. 4th ed. Dubuque: William C. Brown, 1985.

Yamaha Band Instruments Repair Manual

TABLE 1: Everyday Instrument Repairs

Everyday Instrument Repairs: **BRASSES**		
PROBLEM	**POSSIBLE CAUSES**	**SOLUTIONS**
1. Impossible to blow air through the horn--feels as if it is completely stopped up.	a) Valve or valves not clicked in place.	a) Check to see that all valves are clicked in place--try to turn them clockwise; if one turns a little and then locks in place, the problem is probably solved.
	b) Valve or valves in the wrong casing(s).	b) Remove valves and check that the numbers engraved on the valves correspond to the casings. (To prevent mixing up valves in the future, have students oil only one valve at a time and return it to its position before going to the next valve.)
	c) Valve or valves in backwards.	c) Pull out each valve and check that the engraved numbers on the valves all face the same direction. If one is backwards, correct it and try blowing again. The problem may be solved. If all numbers are facing the same direction and no air will blow through the instrument, turn all 3 valves 180 degrees and click in place.
2. Valve makes a clicking sound when pushed.	a) Valve cap is not screwed on completely. The button is hitting the cap when valve is depressed.	a & b) Screw valve caps on completely.
	b) A bottom valve cap is loose.	
3. Fuzzy, airy sound.	a) Water key pad missing or leaking.	a) Replace missing or worn pad--uses a cork or rubber pad. If no cork is available, use whatever will seal off hole (masking tape, a piece of paper) until it can be taken to shop.
	b) Amado type water key (these have a button which is depressed to release the water) is stuck open.	b) Use a small paper clip to pop the button back out on stuck Amado water key.
	c) Tubing has a leak, usually at a soldered joint.	c) Inspect the instrument joints for leaks (tubing may wiggle at the joint, indicating that it has come unsoldered). Use masking tape to seal up the leak until it can be resoldered.

Everyday Instrument Repairs: **BRASSES (continued)**		
PROBLEM	**POSSIBLE CAUSES**	**SOLUTIONS**
4. Valves sticking in place.	a) Dirt and old oil build up.	a) Remove valve. Rinse valve off with water and set aside. Remove top and bottom valve caps and insert cloth through valve casing. Pull cloth back and forth, swabbing out casing. Apply fresh oil to valve and reassemble. (Brass instruments should periodically be given a bath to remove dirt and oil from slides and valves.)
	b) Dented valve or valve casing.	b) Needs to be repaired professionally.
	c) Bent valve slide impinging in valve casing and distorting roundness of casing. Most commonly third valve slide gets bent upward toward bell of trumpet when student knocks the trumpet against the edge of a chair.	c) Trial and error process to determine if slide is bent. Tip off-- bottom or top of slide has a dent. Carefully push valve slide in the direction of the dent (if there is one-- if no dent, pick a direction and try it). If the valve moves more freely, it was bent.
5. Tuning slide stuck in place.	a) Lack of lubrication and build up of dirt.	a) Thread a handkerchief or cloth through the slide loop, giving it a few twists to hold on to the slide. Holding the instrument firmly, give the cloth a sharp tug. (Pull in a direction parallel to the straight tubing on the slide.) Repeat. The sudden jerks should break the slide free. Clean and lubricate before reinserting.
	b) Dented slide	b) Do not pull. Send to repair shop.
6. Valve button and stem wobble drastically--seems as if they have broken off.	Valve button and stem have come unscrewed from the valve.	Remove valve cap. (Button and stem will pull off with it.) Pull remainder of valve from casing and screw together. Reinsert.
7. Mouthpiece stuck in place.	Instrument was dropped or student thumped on mouthpiece while it was in the instrument.	Use a mouthpiece puller--can be purchased commercially--to remove the mouthpiece. Do not try to twist off. If no mouthpiece puller, allow the instrument to cool off, then try again by hand.

Everyday Instrument Repairs: **BRASSES (continued)**		
PROBLEM	**POSSIBLE CAUSES**	**SOLUTIONS**
8. Instrument makes a rattle or buzzing sound when played.	a) A soldered joint has come loose.	a) Needs to be professionally repaired. Can tape over the joint as a temporary solution.
	b) Paper or other foreign object is inside the instrument.	b) Remove slides and valves. Check for paper or other object inside the instrument. Use a cleaning snake to snake out the tubing. (A snake cannot go around the bend in the valve slides--use a pipe cleaner or run water through the tubing to remove a stuck object.)
	c) A valve cap is loose.	c) Tighten valve cap.
9. A valve that was removed from the casing will not go back in completely. Seems to get stuck before the last half inch goes into the casing (primarily on baritone or tuba).	a) Some brass instruments have a small valve guide (star, spur) attached to the valve; this lines up with a notch in the casing, making it easy to insert the valve properly. The guide sometimes comes loose and turns a little from its regular vertical position, making it impossible to insert the valve.	a) With your finger, push the valve guide to its regular vertical position. Insert valve into casing, ensuring that the valve guide lines up with the notch in the valve casing. Have professionally repaired when you can.
	b) There is a dent in the valve casing.	b) Have professionally repaired.
10. Valve does not spring back up when it is depressed and released.	a) Valve lacks lubrication, or dirt and old oil are gumming up the works.	a) Remove valve. Rinse old oil off with water. Dry and lubricate. Reinsert in the instrument to see if the problem is solved.
	b) Valve spring is missing or weak.	b) Look in the case and on the floor for the missing valve spring if none is in the instrument. Add new life to a weakened spring by stretching it out a little and then compressing it.
	c) Valve is binding due to a dent in the casing.	c) Pull valve up manually to see if it binds. If so, have professionally repaired. If not, it's probably a missing spring.

Everyday Instrument Repairs: **BRASSES (continued)**		
PROBLEM	**POSSIBLE CAUSES**	**SOLUTIONS**
11. Valve bounces when springing back up after being depressed. Horn may feel stuffy to blow, but air is going through the instrument.	a) Valve spring is compressed--holes in valve are not lining up properly with tubing. b) Felt pads underneath valve caps are worn too thin to absorb upshock.	a) Stretch spring a little. b) Have felt pads replaced every year.
12. Valve caps are impossible to unscrew.	Build up of grime and years of disuse have caused them to freeze in place.	Use pliers to turn the frozen cap--place a cloth around the cap first to avoid scratching the metal. Use just enough force to prevent the pliers from slipping.
■ **FRENCH HORN**		
13. Valve lever is obviously disconnected from the valve mechanism.	Broken valve string.	Replace broken string. I suggest looking at one of the other strung valves as a reference. The diagram in Figure 2 may help.

FIGURE 2: French Horn Valve Stringing

④ Loosen stop arm screw.
Wrap string around and under it.
Hold key level.
Tighten screw.

③ Insert string through hole.

⑤ Insert string through hole.

② Tie a large knot.

① Start here.

⑥ Loosen string screw.
Twist string end under the loop.
Pull loop tight under string screw and tighten screw.

14. French horn valve lever hits against the horn with a loud click.	a) Valve string is too loose or improperly strung. b) Lever is bent.	a) Re-string, making sure that string is pulled taut. b) Carefully bend back a bent valve lever.
15. French horn pitches are incorrect when either the first or third valves are depressed.	First and third valve slides have been switched.	Check to see that the slide with the longest tubing is connected to the third valve. Reinsert slides in the proper positions.

Everyday Instrument Repairs: **BRASSES (continued)**		
PROBLEM	**POSSIBLE CAUSES**	**SOLUTIONS**
■ **TROMBONE**		
16. Trombone slide catches and sticks in place when played in first position.	Outer slide may be on upside down, causing the lock to catch.	Check that the outer slide is on correctly--the water key should be at the bottom of the slide's curve.
17. Trombone slide will not move easily.	a) Lacks lubrication or is dirty.	a) Lubricate. If that doesn't work, wash off the old oil and grime and apply new oil.
	b) May have a dent.	b) Have professionally repaired.

Everyday Instrument Repairs: **WOODWINDS**		
PROBLEM	**POSSIBLE CAUSES**	**SOLUTIONS**
I. Instrument sounds a different pitch from the one being fingered. Tone quality is normal.	a) Detached spring	a) Look at keys to see if one stays down when others are up. If so, and it offers no resistance when pulled up, turn the instrument over and examine the spring that operates that key. If spring is unattached at one end, use your finger, or a crochet hook, to pop spring back into place (Most keys have a small bracket attached; the bracket has a notched groove into which the spring fits.)
	b) Missing spring	b) Have spring replaced (easy to do, but unless you have the correct-gauge wire, pliers, and time, have it professionally repaired. In an emergency, loop a rubber band over the key in such a way that it acts as a spring; attach to a fixed point on the instrument.
	c) Missing pad	c) Replace pad. Use quick drying pad cement or melt stick shellac. If you still have the old pad and it has shellac on the back, place it in the key cup and heat the cup with a match or lighter. (Be careful not to burn the instrument.) Hold key closed with thumb until pad is in place.
	d) See specific instrument	

Everyday Instrument Repairs: **WOODWINDS (continued)**		
PROBLEM	**POSSIBLE CAUSES**	**SOLUTIONS**
2. Instrument will not blow. No sound of air blowing through instrument.	a) Cleaning swab or other object is stuck in the instrument.	a) Remove object. Some swabs are designed to be stored inside the instrument when put away in the case. Students frequently forget to remove them before playing.
	b) Reed is too soft or is warped and sealing off the mouthpiece.	b) Try a new reed. Check the number printed on the back to be sure it is appropriate for the student.
3. Fuzzy, stuffy, airy tone quality.	a) Bad reed (or incorrect reed placement) on a reed instrument.	a) Replace broken or warped reed; realign crooked reed.
	b) A pad is leaking.	b) Look at the pads to see if they are frayed. (Pads are made of felt with a skin covering. When the skin tears, the pad no longer seals the hole completely.) When one pad is that worn, there will probably be others that are in bad condition. Replace worn pads.
	c) A key is out of adjustment, causing a leakage of air.	c) Look closely at the tone holes when keys are depressed. Are there any places where you can see a space between the pad and tone hole? Many keys operate other keys; the leaky key is often one that is not directly pushed, but is instead operated by another key. Flutes have adjustment screws to keep these co-dependent keys opening and closing the correct amounts. Find the adjustment screw controlling the leaky key, and experiment by turning the screw slightly to see if the leak disappears. On woodwinds, cork bumpers often regulate key height and control the operation of co-dependent keys. Look for a missing or worn cork bumper in the linkage between two keys which would result in one key's leaking.
	d) On a flute, the head joint cork may be loose, allowing air to leak. Notes in the upper and lower ends of the range are then particularly difficult to blow.	d) Try to turn end cap on head joint. If it rotates without ever tightening and offers little or no resistance, cork is too loose. Remove end cap and push cork out the bottom end of

Everyday Instrument Repairs: **WOODWINDS (continued)**		
PROBLEM	**POSSIBLE CAUSES**	**SOLUTIONS**
		head joint, using your finger or the tuning rod. Remove screw and washers from cork, place cork upright on table, and squeeze cork against the table with the heel of your hand. This should plump up the cork. (Pressing it in a vice is even better if one is available.) Reassemble cork, screw and washers and push cork back up into head joint, through the bottom end of head joint. Using a dowel with a slightly smaller diameter than the head joint is recommended when reinserting the cork to evenly distribute the force. To properly position cork, insert bottom end of tuning rod into head joint and adjust cork until tuning mark on rod is centered in blow hole. A coat of Vaseline or even a layer of tape can seal off a leaky cork in an emergency; however the problem usually occurs gradually and worsens over time.
4. Keys make an annoying sticking sound when the instrument is played (especially on flutes).	Build up of dirt and saliva on pads.	Insert a piece of paper (some suggest a dollar bill and others suggest cigarette paper--I use any paper that is handy) between the pad and the tone hole. Depress the key and pull out the paper. Repeat several times, if necessary. This solution is temporary --the pads may need more extensive cleaning. A small amount of rubbing alcohol may be used to wipe off the pad, but this can dry out the pad.
■ **FLUTE**		
5. G# key remains open when its lever is not being pushed.	Bent G# key lever is binding on one of the neighboring keys.	Carefully bend the key lever back so that it completely clears the two neighboring keys when depressed. Remind student not to store pencils or other objects in case because this is a frequent cause of bent keys, as is dropping the flute. The bent G# key is common on flutes.

Everyday Instrument Repairs: **WOODWINDS (continued)**		
PROBLEM	**POSSIBLE CAUSES**	**SOLUTIONS**
■ **CLARINET**		
6. Stuck swab	Swab may be stuck on the speaker tube that sticks out inside the clarinet's upper joint.	Push swab back out the way it came in--a baton works great for this. (A screwdriver or other long tool will work also--be careful not to scratch the inside of the clarinet.)
7. Notes fingered with the right hand do not sound the correct pitch. The rings around the tone holes will not go down completely when pushed (or, just the opposite, the rings stay in the depressed position even when not being pushed).	Bridge key between the upper and lower joints is misaligned or bent. Students frequently are careless when assembling these joints; consequently the bridge gets bent often. Sometimes students even manage to get the lever on the upper joint underneath that on the lower joint.	Check the bridge mechanism to see that the two pieces are properly aligned. Often a simple twist of the upper and lower joints is all that is needed. If a bent lever is preventing keys from closing all the way, use pliers to gently bend the lever to its proper position. Test to see that all keys controlled by the bridge mechanism now close properly. If the lower joint key rings are remaining down even when not being pushed, the student has probably managed to get the lever on the upper joint wedged beneath the lower joint lever (the assembly should be just the opposite.) Carefully untwist the two joints and check for a resulting bent bridge key.
■ **CLARINET OR OBOE**		
8. A wooden clarinet or oboe has a crack.	Natural tendency of wood to shrink and swell with temperature and humidity changes.	Have cracks pinned by a professional repairman. Instruct student on care of a wooden instrument--i.e., do not place on radiators, allow it to gradually change temperatures, etc.
9. Joints of a clarinet or oboe come apart too easily--maybe fall apart without warning. Tone quality is airy.	Missing or worn tenon corks causing air leakage and loose joints.	Have tenon corks professionally replaced. The cork replacement is easy to do, but too time consuming for most school band directors.

Everyday Instrument Repairs: **WOODWINDS (continued)**		
PROBLEM	**POSSIBLE CAUSES**	**SOLUTIONS**
■ SAXOPHONE		
10. Low register will not play; when a low note is fingered, it sounds as a high note.	Octave key is bent, causing the key to remain slightly open even when lever is not pushed.	Hold octave key cup closed with thumbs; gently bend the loop of the octave key mechanism toward the cup, using first two fingers. Check to see if octave key will now close. (Be careful not to bend the octave key mechanism too far or the opposite problem will result: the octave key will not open even when lever is pushed.)
11. G and G# sound the same.	G# key pad is sticking to the rim of the tone hole, preventing it from lifting when G# key is depressed.	Lift the G# key with your finger to break the seal. It should not stick again during that playing session. Saxophone players should get in the habit of checking that key before beginning to play.
12. Low Eb key remains open after key lever is released (or low C does not reopen completely after being released)	The C or Eb key cup is hitting and binding on the metal cage around the cup. The cage has probably been dented.	Bend cage back to prevent binding (or, in an emergency, just remove the cage, but be careful that clothes don't get caught in those keys). The bent cage is usually the result of a drop; chances are that the instrument is also dented where the cage attaches. Have the dented instrument professionally repaired.

Everyday Instrument Repairs: **PERCUSSION**		
PROBLEM	**POSSIBLE CAUSES**	**SOLUTIONS**
■ SNARE DRUM		
1. A head needs to be replaced.	Damaged or worn head.	I strongly recommend using plastic heads for elementary school. (If using calfskin, the procedure is much more complicated, involving soaking and tucking the head. If you choose calfskin, follow the directions in a comprehensive repair guide.) For plastic heads, loosen tensioning rods, remove drum rim, replace damaged head with new head and reassemble drum. Use the following steps for proper tensioning of head.

Everyday Instrument Repairs: **PERCUSSION (continued)**		
PROBLEM	**POSSIBLE CAUSES**	**SOLUTIONS**
2. Tone of drum is poor--tubby or dull sounding.	a) Head tension requires adjustment.	a) If there is more than a little give when you press into the center of the drum head, the head needs tightening (if no give, loosen head). With snares off, tap the batter head in front of each tension rod--tone and timbre should be identical at each rod. Tighten or loosen rods, using a drum key, as needed. Do the same on the snare (bottom) head. Tension on the snare head should be a little looser than on the batter head.
	b) Muffler is too tight.	b) Loosen muffler by turning large screw on side of drum shell.
	c) Snares are damaged or misadjusted.	c) Check snares to make sure that they are in good shape and that they lie flat against the bottom head when on. Adjust if necessary.
■ **BASS DRUM**		
3. A head needs to be replaced or adjusted.	a) Head is torn or worn.	a) Follow directions for replacing snare drum heads.
	b) Tone of drum is unacceptable due to improper tensioning.	b) Follow directions for tensioning snare drum heads. As with the snare, the batter head should be tighter than the opposite head.
■ **CYMBALS**		
4. Cymbal grips need replacement	Worn or broken grips resulting from normal wear and tear.	Cymbal grips are tied using a specific knot (Figure 3). Each leather strap is split in half at each strap. 1) Spread straps out into a + shape. 2) Take strap A and fold it downward over strap B. 3) Fold strap B over strap C, crossing over strap A in the process. 4) Fold strap C over D and B in this same manner. 5) Fold strap D over C and through the loop made by strap A. 6. Pull tight.
5. Cymbal is cracked.	Cymbal was dropped or misused.	Have professionally repaired.

FIGURE 3: Cymbal Strap Knot

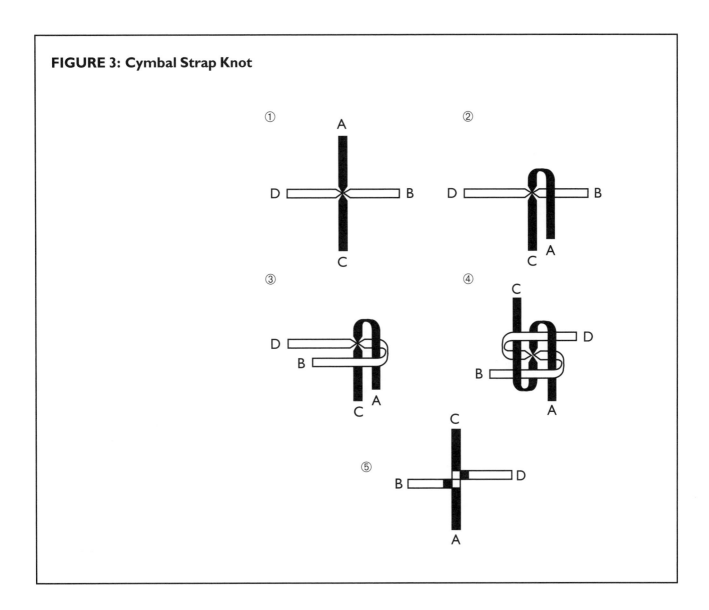

Grading

E ach school system has its own set of guidelines for grading and reporting to parents. Familiarize yourself with this procedure early on. In some schools, students receive letter grades for band; in other schools they receive O (outstanding), S (satisfactory) or U (unsatisfactory). Some schools require two grades, one for effort and one for achievement; others require no grades. Whatever your situation, it is wise to have an established system for determining grades. These days teachers frequently must defend their grade decisions—grades which are wholly subjective or unsubstantiated are difficult to defend.

CRITERIA FOR BASING GRADES

I give students a grade in each of the four following categories; I average these to determine the overall grade:

Performance

This grade will be the average of a number of performance grades recorded throughout the marking period. These performance grades may be from formal playing tests or from informal playing situations.

Practice Cards

A weekly practice card grade is recorded. I ask students to practice for twenty minutes a night or 140 minutes per week, spread over a minimum of five days each week. Students hand in practice cards which are signed by parents. Practice times that fall within various time ranges warrant different grades. These grades are averaged for an overall practice card grade at the end of the marking period. (See sample practice cards—Appendix D.)

All students are expected to attend band, with instruments, each week. If a student forgets his instrument, I mark that with a small circle next to the day's attendance. All students start out with the highest possible grade in this category; the grade is lowered by unexcused absences or repeated forgetting of instruments.

Attendance With Equipment

This category is the most subjective, but it is important to me as it gives students credit for their efforts. Is the student cooperative and attentive in class? Does the student try? Some students who have difficulty with performance put forth a great effort; other students who are extremely talented are disruptive or uncooperative in class. I feel that these are important factors to consider in determining grades.

Effort/Participation

Many directors attach a band progress report to each student's report card. The progress report can address the student's strengths and weaknesses in a way that the quarter grade cannot. A negative aspect of the progress report is the time it consumes. If you decide to use the progress report format, the following areas should be included for evaluation:

PROGRESS REPORTS

- Hand/instrument position
- Knowledge of fingerings
- Dexterity
- Tone production
- Breathing
- Articulation
- Understanding of musical notation
- Understanding of rhythms
- Ability to perform assignments
- Further comments
- Suggestions for improvement ■

Becoming An Integral Part Of The School

For the elementary band teacher who may be in a school only one day a week or less, it is often difficult to become a part of the school. The band director may rarely have the opportunity to talk to other teachers, may be unable to attend faculty meetings and therefore miss out on important information, and may feel like an outsider. Due to the obscurity of the director, the band may attract so little attention that teachers and students seldom think of it except for that one day a week when it creates a temporary diversion. Despite the difficulty of running a band program while less than full time at one school, it is possible to generate interest and enthusiasm which will carry on even in your absence, bringing the band to the forefront of school activities and thoughts.

PERFORMANCE Certainly the best way to attract interest in the band is to perform often. Students love to perform for their classmates, teachers, siblings, and parents, and a performance is a valuable learning experience for students. I grab every opportunity that I can to have the band (or any part of the band) perform. The students perform at various school assemblies, at one or two evening concerts during the year, at a school picnic in the spring, and as a pep band at an outdoor Olympics day organized by the Physical Education department. Groups of students perform on a school recital, at a fine arts night program, and as background for school plays or units. I will often take a class of band students into the office for an impromptu performance of one or two selections. The office staff and administrators enjoy hearing the performances and reward the students' efforts with much praise and enthusiasm. The kindergarten classes make a wonderful audience as well; they are fascinated by the instruments and by the older students. I have often taken a band class into a kindergarten classroom to serenade the students. Both the listeners and the performers benefit from the experience, and the band benefits from the exposure.

Another way to bring the band program to the school's attention is to put up a bulletin board or a display in a prominent location. If the school has a glass case, ask for permission to decorate it one month. You can use instruments, pictures of instruments, sheet music, a music stand—be creative. A bulletin board in the cafeteria can be attention-grabbing. One that showcases the students who are in the band will create pride among the band students and interest among the rest of the students. The following is a possible idea for a bulletin board display:

DISPLAYS

FIGURE 4: Bulletin Board

The staff can be made of thick black yarn or black tape. The music notes, cut out of construction paper, can have band students' names on them and be of different colors, depending on each student's instrument. A color key gives passersby a means of determining who plays what instrument. It is a fun and eye-catching advertisement for the band.

Bulletin board sets can also be purchased at teacher stores and through music novelty catalogs. These sets contain colorful posters and are easy to put up quickly. One music teacher in my school has a "Name the Composer" bulletin board. A frame is attached to the bulletin board and a composer's picture is slipped behind it. Each morning a clue about that composer's life is given over the loudspeaker during the morning announcements. Students can turn in their written guesses to the music teacher, and the first one to identify the composer wins a prize. This competition is usually held during Music in the Schools Month.

ANNOUNCEMENTS

Mentioned in the previous section, announcements can certainly help to showcase your band program. You can phone in your announcement from another school, and without your even being present, your school will be thinking about the band. I use announcements to recognize students' achievements and to remind students about upcoming events, deadlines, or schedule changes. As illustrated by the "Name the Composer" game, announcements can be fun and educational while creating interest in the program.

INVOLVEMENT OF TEACHERS

Involving the classroom teachers in the band program can contribute to the band's popularity and position in the school. Without the support of the classroom teacher, even the most dedicated band director is doomed. Teachers influence their students, consciously or unconsciously. If teachers view band as a positive experience, their students are likely to do the same. The cooperation of the classroom teacher is important in determining and following a schedule and in providing flexibility for students to participate in the band program. I believe that the best way to win the teachers' support is to involve classroom teachers in the band and to be involved in their programs. Notify them of concerts, recitals, and contests. Put programs in their boxes so that they can see which of their students will participate. Remember to thank them publicly for their support.

Find out which teachers played instruments; invite them to tell the students about their experiences in band. Include them in a bulletin board display—"Teachers Who Played in the Band!" or make up a "match-the-teacher-to-the-instrument" game. Ask for their input when arranging schedules. Be flexible when they have field trips or testing during your time with the students. Support their academic programs through music when you can—if a class is studying a particular country, teach the students some music from that country. If they are doing a production, offer to assist with music.

A school in which the teachers of various disciplines support each other is a positive place to teach. The support of the classroom teachers contributes to the success of the band program.

The best way to become a part of the school is to get involved in its operation. Join a committee, if you have the time. Try to get to know the other teachers. Attend faculty get-togethers. Eat lunch with the other teachers. Often my schedule has been so tight that I have skipped lunch or eaten in my room, causing me to lose contact with my colleagues. I make it a point, whenever possible, to eat with the rest of the faculty.

Sometimes the band teacher is overlooked when bulletins or announcements are put in mailboxes. Ask the office staff to include you when distributing information. If you miss the faculty meetings, ask someone to take notes for you. Join in during special events at the school. Offer to assist with class parties, the book fair, S.C.A. elections, the awards assembly; write a school song or take photographs for the yearbook.

Your involvement in the school in areas outside of band will work to your benefit in running the band program. Children recognize you and look forward to seeing you; they are more apt to sign up for your classes. Your interactions with students who are not in the band provide an opportunity to encourage those students to participate in your program. When teachers and administrators see you supporting the school program, they are more likely to support you. Being part of the school community is rewarding and satisfying for most directors.

PERSONAL PARTICIPATION IN SCHOOL ACTIVITIES

CONCLUSION

If you are willing to invest the extra time and effort required, you can make your band program an integral part of the school. Frequent performances by band students, prominently placed band-related displays or posters, schoolwide band announcements, cooperative involvement with classroom teachers, and participation in various school activities are just a few ways to create interest in the band program. Interest in the band program has many advantages such as increased participation and a stronger foundation for the overall pyramid, as well as financial support from the school. The band program that is an integral part of the school is a source of pleasure and pride to students, their parents, the school staff, and the director. ∎

Annotated Guide to Elementary Sheet Music

Selecting appropriate band music can be difficult for a beginning director. Most first-year teachers are unfamiliar with elementary band literature, having spent the past eight or more years concentrating on high school and college level music. Teacher-training programs often fail to cover adequately the subject of elementary band repertoire; however, you must become knowledgeable in this area to be an effective elementary teacher. With limited money to spend on music, the elementary director cannot afford to select unwisely. Each piece that is purchased must be one that can be used for years to come. The time spent researching the available music is time well spent.

The following annotated list of elementary band music is included to assist the beginning band director who may be trying to stock a school music library or select music for a concert. The works listed here are by no means the only good elementary pieces. There are many. These pieces have worked well with my bands and may provide a starting point. I have classified the music into four categories: "beginning," "advanced-beginning," "intermediate," and "advanced." The beginning pieces are suitable for first-year or second-year players, usually by December. The advanced-beginning pieces are fine for first or second year players. They use familiar rhythm patterns and stay within the note range covered in most first-year books. The intermediate pieces are recommended for average second-year players, and the advanced pieces for strong second-year players—perhaps an area band consisting of the top second-year students. Each director's unique situation naturally affects the choice of sheet music. A director whose low brass players are weak may stay away from music (i.e., Trombone Boogie) that features those students. Another director may be fortunate enough to have many, good, low brass players and would like to showcase them. You must make your choices based on your unique situation.

Many other resources are available to assist the director in selecting elementary band music. Annotated listings of new music appear in professional journals such as The Instrumentalist, and this would be an additional source to check. Another good resource is the local music vendor, provided that the store has a large supply of music in stock. I spend several full days each year browsing through music at the dealer's. I believe that this is the best way to become familiar with the available literature.

Music education conferences provide excellent opportunities for examining sheet music: they almost always include exhibits where the latest sheet music is displayed. Teachers can study the music of many different publishers at the conference. Sample tapes of the new music and sample conductors' scores are generally available for interested directors. By putting your name on a mailing list, you can continue to receive recordings and information about new releases throughout the year. Finally, colleagues are a wonderful resource. Most directors are happy to help a fellow teacher by recommending music titles. I like to exchange conductor's scores with other directors—we each benefit from the other's recommendations. If you know of a nearby director who has a good collection of music, ask if you can drop by and browse through the music library. Before long, new directors will be asking for your recommendations on music selection.

Two important tips to keep in mind when selecting sheet music are as follows:

1) Avoid pop tunes that will quickly become dated. A major hit one year fades into obscurity by the next year; you may never play it again. I have four sets of Gloria Estefan's *Rhythm is Gonna Get You* in the back of my file cabinet. The space that it takes up is now more valuable than the music.

2) Buy more parts than you think you will need. Your band may be larger in future years and you will need those parts.

BEGINNING | *Let's Go Band*—**Andrew Balente** (Warner Brothers). The all-time favorite of every elementary band student. If you can buy only one piece of music, this should be it. A spin-off of the University of Michigan fight song, "Let's Go Blue." Requires students to know about seven notes corresponding with the notes covered in the first pages of most method books. Basic rhythms. Good teaching vehicle for accents, staccatos, and repeat signs. Students shout "Let's Go Band!" at the end. I've had students join the band just to play this piece of music.

Fanfare March—**Frank Erickson** (Belwin). A perfect march for first-year students. Playable after only a few months of instruction. Requires students to know about six notes. Basic rhythms. Clarinets stay below the break. Easy trumpet section soli lasting one measure and recurring throughout the piece. Full sounding—even a weak band sounds impressive.

Theme from Beethoven's Ninth Symphony—**Beethoven/arr. John Kinyon** (Alfred). Another very easy yet impressive-sounding piece. Children recognize and enjoy the "Ode to Joy" tune. Easy bass line stays primarily on two pitches throughout most of the piece. Brief clarinet/saxophone soli section and low winds soli section. First clarinets play above the break while seconds play below. An excellent classical selection for an early concert.

Safari—**James Ployhar** (Belwin). Recently back in print. Very easy to put together on short notice. Uses standard notes and rhythms covered early in most method books. Tambourine, timpani, and tom-tom add a Middle Eastern flavor and a driving rhythm to the piece. Dated instrumentation— parts for E flat horn and D flat piccolo are included, but can be disregarded; first, second, and third parts for trumpet, clarinet, and trombone (though second and third parts are often identical). Children and audiences seem to like it.

Changing of the Guard—**Frank Erickson** (Belwin). Based on familiar melodies from London—"London Bridge" and Big Ben's chime. Arranged to sound complete with limited instrumentation. Prominent percussion parts. One low brass/low woodwind soli section. Melody is passed between sections. Sounds good.

Latin Trumpets—**Mike Story** (Belwin). A good Latin-style piece for beginners. Features trumpets, in unison throughout, repeatedly playing the "Mexican Hat Dance" melody. Other instruments are primarily background, but have tuneful parts. Unison clarinet part—stays below the break. Percussion parts include claves, maracas, snare, and bass.

Marines' Hymn—**Traditional/Arr. Jack Bullock** (Belwin). Good arrangement—makes an excellent concert opener. Full-sounding even with limited instrumentation. Brief introduction leads into the familiar tune. Brief low brass/low woodwind soli section. Bass line jumps around somewhat, making it the most challenging of the band parts. Easy to prepare quickly.

ADVANCED–BEGINNING

Trombone Boogie—**Kenneth Henderson** (Belwin). Terrific piece for featuring low brass section. The "boogie theme" (a walking bass line), played by trombones, baritones, and bass clarinets, is challenging but fun for the low brass players who rarely get the melody; other parts are easy. Out of date in its allotment of parts per set—order extra alto sax parts if you have more than three players.

Young America March—**John Kinyon** (Alfred). A wonderful elementary march. Full-sounding and exciting. Several trumpet soli sections throughout the piece. Difficult percussion part for beginners—frequently playing offbeats. Woodwind parts are more technical than other works in this section, but students rise to the challenge because they like this piece. Good piece for teaching several concepts—"D.S. al fine," staccatos, ties, and slurs.

Pomp and Circumstance—**Edward Elgar/Arr. John Kinyon** (Alfred). A nice arrangement of the familiar tune. Features clarinets in large soli section—clarinets stay below the break. Lengthy rest for most other instruments—can be a negative, but my students didn't mind. Easy low brass/low woodwind parts. With exception of four measure introduction, very easy to prepare on short notice. Nice to program on a spring concert when recognizing sixth graders.

Move It—**Nicholas Forte** (Forte). This piece is full of energy. Dynamic opening. A combination of rock and jazz styles. Reinforces several musical concepts—accent, cap accent, crescendo, staccato, repeat signs. Parts are easy and repetitive. No soli sections. Optional drum set part.

Rap it Up—**Ralph Gingery** (William Allen). A rap song for band—truly unique! Comes with prerecorded accompaniment tape which is used in performance. Students alternately play instruments and join in on the rap (which has to do with band—i.e., "We are the band and we came to say we can play with the best of them any day. . ."). Offers many possibilities for creativity. My students auditioned to be rappers—they choreographed moves, dressed for the part, and really added to the piece. Requires a good sound system so that the band can hear and stay with the accompaniment tape. Kids love it. A different piece, *Hoedown*, is printed on the flip side of the sheet music—it's not as interesting as *Rap it Up*, but it could be fun for use in class.

A Touch of Sousa—**Ray Shahin** (Belwin). Based on a theme from Sousa's *Washington Post March*. Sounds great! A little more difficult technically than others listed here (some eighth-note runs), but fits together easily. A nice way to introduce elementary students to Sousa.

Anasazi—**John Edmondson** (Queenwood). Name is derived from that of an ancient Indian tribe. Music fits the title. Very easy, low brass ostinato part reminiscent of Indian drums. Calls for bass drum, tom-tom, woodblock, and tambourine—easy rhythms. Many scale-wise passages for woodwinds. Alto saxophone parts are rather low for beginners. Some unusual harmonies—good for broadening elementary students' musical tastes.

INTERMEDIATE | *Rudolph the Red-Nosed Reindeer*—**Johnny Marks/Arr. John Kinyon** (Alfred). A nice arrangement of the popular Christmas song. Trumpets have the main theme throughout. Easy and fun low brass part. Brief clarinet soli section. Children love to play it and to hear it performed.

Christmas Chimes—**Traditional/Arr. John Kinyon** (Alfred). A wonderful arrangement of the *Ukranian Bell Carol (Hark How the Bells)*. More technical for woodwinds than most pieces listed, but repetitious—mine loved the challenge. Low brass parts pose no problems. All sections get a chance to shine and have interesting parts.

Frosty the Snowman—**Steve Nelson and Jack Rollins/Arr. Michael Sweeney** (Hal Leonard). My favorite of several available arrangements. Nice piece to end a winter concert. More difficult low brass parts than most—brief soli section. Melody dove-tails between various instruments. Full-sounding.

Festival of the Eternal Lights—**Traditional/Arr. Clark Tyler** (Alfred). A great Hanukkah piece. Most students recognize and enjoy the tune. Another technical piece for woodwinds and high brass, but tempo is flexible. Easy low brass part. Separate woodwind and brass soli sections. Builds in intensity to an exciting climax.

The Blue Rock—**Dale Lauder** (Alfred). A favorite of all band students. The piece really rocks. Range is high for some players—first trumpets play up to high E flat and flutes play up to high D flat. Catchy rock theme is passed off to all sections. Low brass part is fun and fairly easy—one soli section. May look difficult to students at first glance (page is crowded), but is fairly repetitive. They'll quickly master it.

The Star-Spangled Banner—**Francis Scott Key/Arr. John Kinyon** (Alfred). Great for special school functions. Sounds full and impressive. Flutes and first trumpets in high register—may need to teach some fingerings. Low brass part jumps around and contrasts rhythmically with the rest of the band, making it difficult for those students to play. Need good cymbals—exciting part.

The Silver Scepter—**John Kinyon** (Alfred). A terrific concert overture for elementary students. Dramatic opening. Several tempo and style changes. Slow and stately in places, quick and bouncy in others. Great for teaching many new concepts and terms: "maestoso," "tempo primo," "allegretto," triplets, staccatos, fermata, ritard. Unison clarinet soli section—low register. Sounds impressive.

Celebration—**James Ployhar** (Belwin). An exciting medley of tunes from various holidays tied together with an original theme by Ployhar. Familiar tunes included are "Yankee Doodle," "Jingle Bells," and "Happy Birthday." Dotted quarter notes occur frequently, sometimes causing counting problems. Some chromatic passages in inner voices. Impractical instrumentation for most elementary school bands—separate trombone and baritone parts; most sections divided between first, second and third parts. Many parts are doubled, so it still sounds fine with incomplete instrumentation.

ADVANCED

Evening at the Symphony—**Sandy Feldstein and John O'Reilly** (Alfred). Another medley—this time of famous symphonies. Included are passages from Beethoven's ninth and fifth symphonies, Haydn's *Surprise Symphony,* and Mozart's *Eine Kleine Nachtmusik.* Trumpet parts are very high for elementary students—they enter on high E—but parts can be played an octave lower. Technically challenging. Children and parents recognize and enjoy the pieces.

Meadowlands—**James MacBeth** (Alfred). A great festival piece for an area band. A challenging grade II in Virginia. Russian in style—heavy driving rhythms. Heavily accented. Need strong trumpeters. High brass parts. Bass clarinet soli section. Brief trumpet solo. Builds in intensity as each section enters. Challenging percussion parts. Dramatic climax.

Wipe Out—**The Surfaris/Arr. Eric Osterling** (Warner Brothers). A good band arrangement of a classic rock and roll tune that is still popular with children. Percussion feature—requires solid drummers. Optional drum set part. Some tricky syncopated rhythms in all parts. Difficult, but my area band students beg to play it each year.

Discovery Band Book—**John Edmondson and Anne McGinty** (Hal Leonard). A collection of fifteen Discovery Band pieces that were once available separately. Good variety. Has *Frosty the Snowman* (more difficult than that listed earlier), *Grandfather's Clock, Jingle-Bell Rock, Super-Flutes, Breakdance Brass,* a few marches and more. ■

Performance Suggestions

Most beginning elementary band directors approach their band's first public performance with some trepidation. Ironically, the musical aspect of the performance is often the least of their worries—it is the numerous, seemingly insignificant details involved in giving a performance that create stress. Being solely responsible for the actions and performance of a large group of children can be debilitating or, if approached correctly, can be exhilarating. The key to a successful elementary band performance is planning. The following ideas may help to make your concert the success that it can be.

In addition to musically preparing the band for performance, there are a myriad of other concert preparations which the director must oversee. Two important preparations are those of setting a date and obtaining building use. The two are interconnected. Your first step should be to determine on which dates the room is available. Most schools have a building use calendar to facilitate this. It is also wise to check with the junior high and high schools in your pyramid, once you have a date in mind, to avoid scheduling your concert on a night that they have planned a major activity. Parents who have children in different schools in the pyramid would then have a problem, which means that you would also have a problem.

    If the concert is scheduled by the school, perhaps for a P.T.A. meeting, and the band is asked to perform, building use has probably been taken

CONCERT PREPARATIONS

care of; however, if you are running the show on your own (perhaps an area band concert which would not involve the P.T.A.), then you will need to sign out a room. The school cafeteria or gym are the two most likely choices, and both are used frequently for outside activities such as scouts, church, recreation, and so on. School activities generally take precedence, so talk to the person in charge before ruling out a date. You may want to use a separate room for warming up and storing cases. If so, sign the room out.

Another preparation is the printed program. If you are planning to have a typed program, who will type it? At some schools the secretaries handle this, and at others it is the director's job. Either way, the director must make a list of all band students, deciding on an order (alphabetically?, by instrument?, by chairs?) and must know the pieces to be performed as well as composers. It is sometimes difficult to plan the program content and order much in advance since some pieces can be "iffy" right up to the last minute, but it is better to prepare the program and later announce any changes than to wait until the last minute and have to race around to finish the program. My advice in listing your students in the program is to double and triple check that no names are left off. Elementary students are crushed by the omission of their names. I use an alphabetical listing, by instrument, with a symbol next to the names of advanced students. (See sample concert program—Appendix E)

ADVANCE NOTIFICATION

As soon as you have set your concert date, send the information home with students, post it, put it in the school newsletter, prepare reminder notices to go home a day or two before the concert, and realize that you still will not be able to reach every parent. Elementary students are notorious for failing to give parents paperwork from school. The best approach is the "blitz"—broadcast the information in every possible way. Then, three to four weeks before the concert, send home a concert information letter with a detach-and-return section which the parent signs and which states that the parent has received the concert information and will have the child there. I allow about two weeks for students to hand in the signed forms, and I always keep extras on hand because students often lose them. I then call every home from which a form is not returned. I have made as many as fifty to sixty calls out of a band of one hundred fifty children, and I feel that this irresponsibility is a real weakness of many of today's students; however, it is the only way that I have found to ensure that every parent receives the concert information. Often the parent has seen and signed the letter, but the student has forgotten to return it. Too often, though, the parent knows nothing about the concert and so I relay the information over the phone. It matters greatly to me that every student be present for the concert, and so I am willing to do this calling. Other directors may feel that the students need to learn responsibility sometime, and they don't mind using their concert as a vehicle for teaching this. A compromise might be the best solution—make a list of those who have not returned forms and call only a few of the key players (i.e., a tuba or star trumpeter).

In your concert information letter, be sure to include the following: date, time (for the students to report and for the concert to begin), place, dress, and equipment. If you will have any special rehearsals in preparation for the concert, you may want to list those as well. (See sample concert information letter—Appendix G)

I send one final concert reminder letter home a day or two before the concert just to ensure that no one forgets. (See sample concert reminder letter—Appendix H) A word of caution—double and triple check your dates and times on all letters that go home. A mistake in one letter can be a nightmare to try to correct and can jeopardize your concert.

WARMING UP FOR THE CONCERT

I recommend having elementary students arrive about thirty minutes before the concert for warming up and tuning. There is a fine line between enough warming up and too much. Remember that elementary students have limited embouchure endurance; a lengthy warm up could result in worn out lips and cracked notes midway through the concert. I begin with lip slurs for the brass, followed by one or two scales in whole notes during which the students respond musically to the way I conduct (louder if bigger gestures, softer if smaller). This procedure focuses the students and gets them to look up. I then quickly tune the band using a tuner and hearing individuals and sections play four notes (concert F, G, A, Bb). Finally I start each piece in order to keep the tunes in the front of the students' minds.

I find it helpful to have a few classroom teachers stay in the warm-up room to help oversee the students. The individual tuning requires that students sit quietly for several minutes, and this is difficult for excited children. The teachers can be a great help in maintaining order. Be sure to recognize them publicly during the concert!

ANNOUNCEMENTS

When professional conductors walk on stage to conduct symphony orchestras, they do not stop by a microphone to introduce themselves or the group or to explain the program; however, when the elementary band teacher conducts a concert, communication with the audience is appropriate and expected. Many directors are uncomfortable speaking publicly; they may feel more confident referring to notes. Others are able to ad lib. Use the concert as an opportunity to mention upcoming band activities or other information that you want the parents to receive and to publicly recognize students and supporters (i.e., the classroom teachers, the administration, the custodians, parent volunteers). I keep a list in my hand of everything that I want to mention—with so much going on, it is easy to forget your intended announcements.

If you will not have a printed program, then you should announce each selection on the concert. (I strongly recommend having a typed program—parents send it to the relatives, children save it for scrapbooks, and you can use it as a reference in later years.) Even if a printed program is available, briefly telling about the pieces to be performed adds to the audience's enjoyment. You can use this opportunity to tell parents a little about your program, to point out how the music illustrates musical concepts that you have been working on in class, or simply to educate. Two or three sentences is generally sufficient.

An idea that I have found useful is to select student announcers for each piece to be performed. I write out their speeches and select students to read the speeches. I open the concert with a brief introduction and then turn the microphone over to the students. Parents enjoy hearing the students speak, and this allows me the time to prepare myself for conducting the next piece. (I can get up my music, think about the tempo, remind myself of cues that I will give, and so on.) Most students enjoy announcing; the selection of announcers can be a reward for hardworking students. A typical announcement might read as follows:

> Hello. My name is *Mary Smith,* and I play the *flute* in the band. Our next selection on tonight's concert is *The Dragons of Komodo* by *John Kinyon.* The piece is named for the large lizard-like creatures living on the island of Komodo in the South Pacific. These reptiles can grow up to ten feet in length and weigh over two hundred pounds. You are sure to enjoy this exciting piece.

I recommend making your announcements regarding band activities near the end of the concert, perhaps just before the last piece.

While many high school and even junior high bands own uniforms, few elementary schools have funds for this. The director has flexibility in deciding on dress, though the principal may also have an opinion. Many directors prefer their band students to dress in a uniform fashion such as wearing black skirts or slacks with white shirts; other directors prefer to have students wear whatever dress clothes they own. In bands where funds and/or parent volunteers are readily available, sashes, ascots or ties in a school's colors might be an option.

I generally have my students dress uniformly in dark slacks/skirts, white shirts, and ties (boys). I feel that the uniformity contributes to the concept of teamwork among students. At the end of our spring concert I have a photographer take a group photograph, and for this I also prefer the uniform appearance.

Many bands have a set routine for putting instruments up. For example, between pieces the students sit with their instruments on their laps (I refer to this as "resting position"), and when the conductor steps onto the podium, the students put their instruments upright on their knees ("attention position"). The students' instruments go up to their mouths ("playing position") when the conductor's hands go up. This military-style move can create an interesting visual effect and conveys the idea that the band is disciplined and attentive; even more importantly, it focuses the students' attention on the conductor and prepares them mentally for beginning a piece of music. I frequently use this "horns up" routine even in rehearsals because it is so effective for getting the students' attention. I don't move from "attention" to "playing position" until I see that everyone is looking up. I often use that moment, when students are waiting for my hands to go up, to give an instruction during a rehearsal because I know that everyone is paying attention.

In addition to dazzling the audience and helping to focus the students' attention, a "horns up" routine can help build a sense of unity and esprit de corps among the students. My students have told me that they feel proud when they snap their horns to attention as a group. If the move is sloppy in a rehearsal, they will ask to do it again because they know that they can do better. They gain a feeling of group accomplishment and pride in doing it well. Younger students who see the band perform often tell me later that they especially liked it when the band students put their instruments up together. Clearly, the instruments-up routine appeals to children. It can be a useful tool for focusing students' attention, creating a feeling of unity among the band students, and conveying a visual impression to the audience. ■

APPEARANCE OF THE GROUP

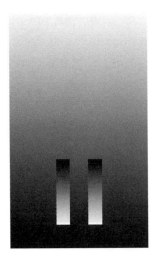

Organizing An Area Band

Directing an area band is a responsibility of many elementary band directors. The area band is an extracurricular performing group made up of students from elementary schools within a particular area. The students may meet once or twice a week to rehearse, and they generally perform several times during the year. Elementary band students benefit musically from the experience of playing in a full ensemble with complete instrumentation. Many smaller elementary schools are unable to provide this full ensemble experience within the school due to their limited enrollment. Area bands provide students in these small school band programs the opportunity to play in a large, properly balanced group.

Participation in area band is often reserved for second-year players. Most directors consider the area band to be an honor band of advanced students; therefore, the music performed should be somewhat more challenging than the regular school band music. Membership can be by audition, by invitation, or by appearance at the first rehearsal. Regardless of the method of determining membership, a fundamental rule must be the requirement of regular attendance. The area band should be an activity to which students look forward; it affords enthusiastic and talented band students the opportunity to play challenging music within a group of other experienced players.

Before band rehearsals can begin, the director must first make a variety of decisions and arrangements. The following are some questions to consider:

PREPARATION

A director who has several schools located near each other may want to group these together. Sometimes two or more directors may wish to combine schools and form a larger jointly run area band. A director whose schools are spread far apart may not be able to combine all schools; in that case, it is sometimes necessary to arrange for students in one or two schools to participate in another director's area band. Bear in mind that the more schools involved in one area band, the fewer students there can be from each school if a standard total enrollment is to be achieved. An enrollment of between sixty and ninety students works well. Larger groups can be unwieldy and less beneficial to the individual students in the ensemble.

What Schools Will I Include In My Area Band?

A centrally located school is one possibility. Some area bands meet at the intermediate or high school in their pyramid. An advantage of this location choice is that the rooms are already set up for rehearsals whereas elementary school cafeterias or gyms are not; directors get tired of lugging equipment out, setting up chairs, and putting things back to normal following rehearsals. Those pressed for time will appreciate the advantages of the intermediate or high school band room. Often the intermediate or high school directors are glad to assist in some capacity—after all, the area band programs ultimately benefit their programs by providing a strong foundation for the students who will one day be theirs. One of my area bands met in the nearby intermediate band room. The director had her last class arrange the chairs according to my seating chart. She allowed us to use all of her percussion equipment—timpani, snare drums, bass drum, xylophone, orchestra bells, tambourines, claves, woodblocks, triangles—which saved me much time and energy. The situation was ideal. Your location will depend upon what is available at the time you choose to have rehearsals. You may expect to complete some type of building-use form or to sign out a room for the duration of your band season.

Where Will The Band Practice?

The answer to this question depends on many factors. How much time beyond regular contract hours are you willing to donate? Do you intend to enter any festivals or competitions with the group? How much time can you expect your students and their parents to dedicate to band? Children today are often involved in so many organized extracurricular activities such as sports, scouts, church, and paper routes that they have little time

How Often Will The Area Band Rehearse?

left for additional activities. With both parents working in many cases, asking for too much of a time commitment can deter participation. Area bands in Fairfax County generally rehearse once, sometimes twice, each week. A few bands attend the district band festival and require the extra rehearsal time to prepare. If I plan to attend the District Festival, my area band meets once a week until January. From January through March we rehearse twice a week, and from March to May we return to one rehearsal a week. If you plan to shift the rehearsal schedule mid-year, be sure to state this in your initial area band informational letter to the parents. Many families will plan their activities around your band schedule if they have the information in time.

When Will The Band Practice?

Many factors may influence your decision regarding rehearsal times. Availability of the rehearsal location is an important determinant. If you will use a junior high or high school building, your schedule must be worked around that school schedule. Some school systems such as Fairfax County have early closings one day each week for teacher planning. Many directors rehearse during this time. It is still contract time, so directors are paid for their work, and it saves teachers who live far away from having to return later for an evening rehearsal. Students' schedules are generally free during those afternoon hours since they are in school at that time during the remainder of the week. The problem of student transportation has increased in the past few years with both parents working. In some areas buses may be available; in other areas, car pools work well. In some areas, evening rehearsals may be the only solution. You must assess your situation and decide what will work best for you and for the community.

How Do I Select And Obtain Music For My Area Band?

The music selected should be slightly more challenging than that for the regular school band. This is a good opportunity to introduce students to music with varying textures such as solo and soli sections as well as other musical concepts beyond the scope of the once-a-week band class. Unfortunately, your selection of music may be influenced by budgetary concerns leaving you with limited choices.

In Fairfax County, each area once handled area band music allocations separately. Now, however, all requests for area band music go through a central music library. Directors are encouraged to sign out sets of sheet music; accurate loan records are kept. The library may order new music at the director's request if funds are available. If your school system has no funds allocated for area band music, you may need to spend your school music budget, if you have one, or request money from the school principal or P.T.A. A supportive principal may contribute to your program from school discretionary funds. If no funds are available for purchasing music, other options include borrowing music from other schools, fund raising, and encouraging donations. These last two ideas should be undertaken only after the approval of your principal. Various school systems may have set policies regarding fund raising and solicitation. Since the music order process may take several weeks to complete, it is wise to select your music well ahead of time and to make whatever arrangements are necessary for obtaining the music.

When selecting area band music, choose pieces that will hold the interest of the students while teaching important musical concepts. See the annotated list of band music for suggestions on music selection. I spend a great deal of time browsing through elementary band music and keeping lists of potential pieces for my school and area bands. Vendors are always present at the various state and national music education conferences held each year; attendance affords an excellent opportunity for previewing the new music that is out. At these conferences you can also put your name on various mailing lists and receive demo tapes and sample scores of new music. Exchanging ideas with other band directors is also wise—some of my favorite pieces for band I ordered at the suggestion of another director. The larger music stores stock much band music and are excellent for browsing as is a central music library.

How Often Will The Band Perform?

Most area bands perform several concerts during the year. A winter concert and a spring concert are standard. Many area bands are more active. Some attend festivals or competitions; some play for community activities such as fairs, parades, grand openings, dedications, or for nursing homes and hospitals. My area band does a winter concert which might include a few holiday tunes, a march or two, and a classical piece. Later we do a festival and a pre-festival concert of all classical music, and we end the year with a concert of lighter, pops-oriented pieces which we perform on a concert tour of the various elementary schools involved. Your decision on the number and types of performances may affect your choice of music and your rehearsal schedule. Once you decide on your performance goals, set concert dates and write them in on your school's calendar.

How Will Membership In The Area Band Be Determined?

Many factors may influence your decision. The number of schools involved can be one factor. If many schools combine to form one band, fewer students from each school can participate. This can be both good and bad. Taking only the strongest players makes for a very high level group; however, you must decide if this approach is best for you and for your students. Certainly the top players benefit from the opportunity to play challenging music with other talented students, but the students who are not selected will be unhappy. Their self esteem and overall interest in band may suffer, lowering morale in your school band. I prefer to combine only a few schools in order to reduce the competition for membership. I view the area band as a means of improving my students' musicianship. Too much selectivity defeats my purpose because only a few students benefit.

On the other hand, being accepted into the area band should be a source of pride to students. If there are no standards for membership, there is no sense of accomplishment. I once taught an area band which was open to anyone who wanted to show up. The students seemed less committed, less serious, more sporadic in attendance, and more lax in their music preparation than students who had had to pass an audition to play in other groups. I recommend requiring the students to pass an audition, even if you plan to take everyone who tries. The students value their membership in the group because they have worked to attain it.

Auditions can be done in a variety of ways. If several schools are involved, all students playing a specific instrument can be scheduled to audition on a certain day and time. The same person can hear and evaluate all auditioners. This is a formal approach and it can be daunting to students, possibly turning some away before they even try; however, if seating according to skill is to be done, the method is fair. I prefer a more casual approach. I co-direct an area band with one other director; we listen to our own students' auditions and then later compare notes. My students audition during band class, and they are not nervous about playing for me since they do it each week anyway. A few other directors have their students participate in our band; they also handle their own auditions and then recommend those students who do well. Taping the auditions can be helpful when different directors will be hearing students audition.

Membership can also be based solely on the director's recommendation. The students may not feel the sense of achievement that comes from passing an audition, but this method has the advantage of requiring the least effort.

Once these preliminary questions have been answered—rehearsal times have been chosen and locations signed out, sheet music has been selected, performance goals have been determined, and membership criteria has been decided upon—you are now ready to begin your area band. Students should be given a letter telling them and their parents about the area band. Include any audition information in this letter as well as rehearsal and concert dates, times, and locations. (See sample area band informational letter—Appendix I)

Complete auditions (if you choose this approach) and notify students of acceptance via a letter. Repeat in this letter all previously stated information such as rehearsal times and location, concert dates and your expectations for the students. (See sample area band acceptance letter—Appendix J)

Have folders filled and ready to distribute at the first rehearsal. Placing name tags on chairs can eliminate much confusion for the first several weeks. The following is a suggested seating arrangement:

BEGINNING YOUR AREA BAND

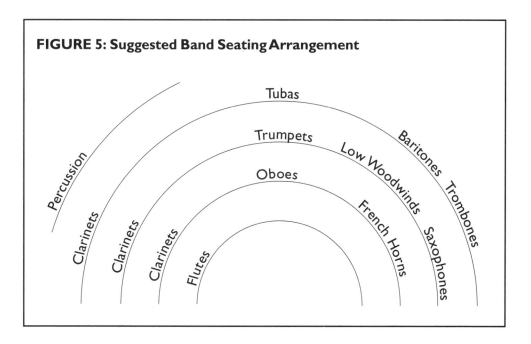

FIGURE 5: Suggested Band Seating Arrangement

You may wish to organize a student set up crew if much equipment needs to be moved to prepare for the rehearsals. Student music librarians can greatly assist the director; students benefit from the leadership opportunity and enjoy the special responsibility.

At the first rehearsal, establish rules. The students who participate in an extracurricular activity such as area band are generally motivated and enthusiastic. They are proud to have been chosen, and discipline is generally no problem; however, all children need to know what you expect of them, so be sure to go over this. You may want to set guidelines for attendance, for behavior during rehearsals, for break-time behavior, for home practice, and for performance.

Establish routines, such as warming up and tuning instruments at the beginning of the rehearsal, and stacking chairs and returning school-owned stands at the end of the rehearsal. I often use lip slurs and/or scales as a warm-up exercise. I might adjust the tempo or style of my conducting, while the students play a slow scale, to focus the band's attention and to get them in the habit of watching me. Once the students and instruments are warmed up, tuning is the next step. I tune the tubas to a tuner and then tune the rest of the band, individually, to the tubas. This tuning-from-the-bottom-up approach gets students used to listening to the tuba, which is important because the tubas pitches are at the bottom of the over-tone series, and the rest of the band needs to match pitches with the over-tones in that series if the band is to sound well in-tune.

Once the necessary organizational steps for forming an area band are completed, the director's real work is done. Such organization ensures productive, rewarding rehearsals and a successful area band program. ■

Maintaining Student Interest

One of the most challenging aspects of elementary band directing is maintaining a high level of student interest throughout the entire year. Any experienced director knows the cycle of student interest only too well: there is unbelievable excitement among the students at the beginning of the year, lasting for about two months, during which there is tremendous individual practice with nearly everyone remembering to come to band prepared with equipment. Many students move ahead in their band books on their own and will ask for extra lessons to get ahead. Students are happy to miss recess or other favorite activities to come to band.

This excitement is followed by a gradual waning of interest once the novelty has worn off—students may begin forgetting their instruments, stop handing in practice cards, need to be reminded to come to band, and ask to be excused from band so as not to miss something of interest in their classrooms. During this period students begin to drop out of the program. The dropping out accelerates. Unwary directors may find their bands crumbling before their eyes.

I make maintaining student interest and enthusiasm a top priority—it is rare that any students drop out during the year or fail to continue for both their fifth and sixth grade years once they begin in band. It requires a conscious effort on the director's part to achieve program stability. The following suggestions may aid beginning band directors in avoiding the unfortunate scenario of band atrophy described above.

PERFORM OFTEN

Frequent performance is the single most important means of maintaining student interest. Students love to perform for anyone who will listen—classmates, teachers, parents, community members. The excitement that is generated by a performance is often enough to reinvigorate those students whose interest is lessening and to maintain the high interest of the other students. In addition to the standard spring concert, you might give a winter concert, have the band perform for a special schoolwide celebration such as arbor day, field day (schoolwide Olympics) or spirit day, or take the band to perform at a nursing home or other community center. Perhaps you can start a tradition at your school—a band ice-cream social or a band performance at the school fair. Have the band perform the national anthem at the awards assembly or at an S.C.A. assembly.

Impromptu performances are equally exciting to students. Take a class to perform for the kindergarten—kindergartners make a wonderful audience—or take a group into the lunchroom to serenade students. Invite the principal or secretaries in to hear a brief performance in class. Accept invitations and look for opportunities to have your students perform—the rewards in terms of maintaining student interest will be well worth the effort.

ESTABLISH A REGULAR ROUTINE

Create a regular routine for your students and stick with it—coming to band class prepared to play on the appropriate day must become part of your students' weekly routines. Consistency is fundamental in establishing any routine. Without regular attendance students cannot progress, and once progress halts, interest is lost. No matter how inconvenient or difficult to schedule it might be, I recommend seeing each student each week. If a holiday falls on your day at one school, try to adjust your schedule at another school to accommodate both groups of students so that no one misses band class. It may mean taking all students together at one school for a full rehearsal, and you may not be able to cover new material in the method book, but, at the least, you will have held your students' ground and conveyed your expectation of regular attendance in the band program.

Band directors lament the fact that their Monday schools are always behind and that it is nearly impossible to maintain interest when weeks at a time pass without seeing the Monday students. There might be a Monday holiday, then a Monday snow day, then the teacher is sick on a Monday, and then the students are away on a field trip—a month passes and the students are out of the habit of coming to band. They have forgotten everything they had learned. Once the novelty of playing the instrument has waned and the initial exuberance is gone, it is a struggle to try to start over if the student falls behind. Most would rather give up than backtrack. For this reason it is crucial that you do not allow the downward spiral to ever begin. Maintaining a regular schedule where students are seen each week is the key. I consider it my chance to give them their weekly dose of invigoration which will carry them through the week of practice until I see them again.

▌BE VISIBLE

It is important to keep the band in the forefront of students' thoughts; not just the band students' thoughts, but those of all students in the school. Visit the classrooms often, as long as the classroom teachers do not object. When I need to make an announcement or remind students of something, I try to go in person rather than leaving a note for the classroom teacher to relay. Students will often ask me questions which I can answer then, and even the nonband students see me so often that they feel as if they know me and I them.

Make schoolwide announcements frequently to congratulate students on accomplishments or to let them know of schedule changes and the like. The announcements familiarize all the students in the school with the activities of the band and can generate interest. Put up posters in the halls or a photo display showing the band's activities. The more the band becomes a focus of positive attention in the school, the more the students want to remain associated with it.

Participate in all aspects of the school program—be involved in your students' overall education. Help out at the book fair, volunteer for bus duty, attend class plays and special events, sponsor a club. There are a million ways in which you can become involved. Not only will your students benefit from your generosity, but you will also benefit: the good will that you foster with the classroom teachers, the P.T.A. and the administration can make your job so much easier in the long run, and the connection that you have with your students will be stronger, increasing your effectiveness as a teacher. Remember that you represent the band, and anything positive that you do for the school reflects well on the band program.

PROVIDE SPECIAL ACTIVITIES

Another excellent means of maintaining student interest is to provide opportunities for students to participate in special activities in addition to the weekly band class. The more involved students become in band activities, the stronger your band program will be.

The solo and ensemble festival is one recommended special activity . It is an extracurricular event in which students can participate if the director is a member of MENC (Music Educators' National Conference). Each state is divided into various districts which set their own dates, but the event usually takes place in April. Many students are eager to prepare music and to attend the festival in the hopes of earning a medal which will later be publicly presented to them at a concert.

About half of my band attends the solo and ensemble festival each year, and some students participate in three or four ensembles. For the few months preceding the festival, the band room is a buzz of excitement with students staying after school or coming in during my breaks for extra help. The level of enthusiasm and of performance rises greatly during what could be a slow couple of months. I often combine an entire class into a large group ensemble such as a beginning clarinet choir; this way many students are involved at once without the stress of performing individually, as in a solo. All of the students in the group can win medals, and this is a strong motivator. Working toward a common goal further unites and strengthens the band, making students feel that they are part of a team.

An optional solo and ensemble recital can be a further motivator. I have so many students asking to perform that I often have to hold it on two separate nights to avoid a marathon-length recital. Students love to perform for their parents and friends, and though they'll deny it, they enjoy dressing up for a special occasion. A small reception after the recital is a nice reward for the students. While helping them over their "butterflies" before the festival, the recital also teaches students proper concert manners (applauding for others, bowing, acknowledging the accompanist), exposes them to a great deal of music literature, and allows them to learn from each other.

Area band is another excellent activity for strong second-year players. It provides an extra challenge for advanced students because they are combined with the top players from other elementary schools. With several concerts presented during the year, the extra performance opportunities make this a strong motivator for students, because almost all children love to perform. I know of one director who created a special area band for first-year players. This is a wonderful opportunity for the students; unfortunately, the director must donate his free time for such an activity and there is a limit to how much even the most dedicated teachers can give.

Other ideas for special band activities might be a band fund-raiser (bake sale, ice-cream social/concert), a field trip to hear a professional performing group, or a concert at the local retirement home. When my band visited the nearby retirement home, the students were excited for weeks ahead of time; that was all that they talked about. "Will we be going to the retirement home again?" was one of the first questions that the students asked the following year. What a great motivator! Other directors take their bands to perform at the local shopping malls for the holidays. This would not be my first choice because of the potential for problems, but the directors and their students who have done this thought it was terrific. One director formed a jazz band with several of her top players and had the group perform on a school band concert. A band party mid-way through the year might be another fun special activity for your students.

Providing special activities for students to take part in outside of the regular band class helps to maintain student interest. Spacing the activities over the course of the year can keep your band in a state of constant anticipation and enthusiasm, thus avoiding the common problem of band attrition.

SELECT MUSIC WITH STUDENTS IN MIND

Music is perhaps the strongest tool a director can use for motivating students. A student once told me that he had signed up for band solely because he wanted to learn to play the song *Let's Go Band* (see Chapter Nine—Annotated Guide to Elementary Sheet Music). Some students have made their choice of instrument based entirely on the song that was used to demonstrate that instrument at the recruitment program. When selecting music, keep your students in mind. While I believe that a diet of only rock or pop music is unbalanced and inadequate, I do suggest selecting some tunes that appeal specifically to students. Try to stay current with students' tastes—they enjoy playing theme music from hit movies or popular television shows, or from a special event such as the Olympics. Most pieces with the word "rock" in the title also appeal to children. There are many excellent pop tunes available, and they can be as effective for teaching musical concepts as the classical pieces.

It may surprise some directors to find that elementary children really do enjoy playing classical pieces—especially those that they recognize. There are some excellent elementary band arrangements of well-known classical works. The John Kinyon Mini-Score Series (Alfred Publishing

Company) contains many. My students love playing the *Theme from Beethoven's Ninth Symphony* (arranged by John Kinyon and better known as *Ode to Joy*) and *Evening at the Symphony* (arranged by Feldstein and O'Reilly—a medley of famous works by Beethoven, Haydn and Mozart). While children *love* to play familiar pieces, they *hate* playing simplified pieces that have been arranged in such a way that the basic rhythm or tune that they expect to hear is altered. Your students will either drive you crazy by playing it the way they have heard it, or you will drive them crazy by making them play what is written.

When selecting music, try to choose a variety of styles—some marches, some classical, some popular, some folk songs, and some novelty pieces. You might even try your hand at composing: children are enthusiastic about playing music that you have written just for them. I wrote a simple piece titled *The Cherry Run March,* and it quickly became a favorite of the students. They seemed flattered that I would write a piece for them.

Novelty pieces can often provide students an opportunity to express their creativity with props or costumes or with a choreographed activity. For example, when my band played the *Theme from Jeopardy* on a concert one year, a brief skit accompanied the performance: students had constructed and decorated podiums behind which the contestants stood, and one student was dressed as a game show host and read the clue (i.e., "This Fairfax County elementary school has the best students, teachers, administrators, and parents in the world"). The two contestants scratched their heads while the band played, then held up their cards which read "Cherry Run" when the song finished. It was a big hit, and the ideas came from the students. When my band performed Ralph Gingery's *Rap it Up*, students auditioned to be rappers, choreographed moves and coordinated their clothing for an exciting performance. They knew better than I what would be appropriate for that type of music, and the result was fantastic. If you give your students the opportunity, they may give you some excellent ideas for performances; at the same time, the students are being highly motivated by the music.

In addition to motivating students through band music, I try to keep on hand materials for those students who need additional resources—i.e., books with music from popular children's movies such as *Beauty and the Beast* or *The Little Mermaid,* as well as books with television show themes, pop songs, folk songs, and patriotic songs. I sign the books out for a week at a time and am always adding to my collection. My students can't wait to take the books home so that they can play these favorite songs for their parents. They are strongly motivated by the music. Music, when selected with your students in mind, can be a director's best motivational tool; it should be chosen with care and consideration.

Someone once said that "timing is everything," and this is never more true than in the field of elementary band directing. Knowing in advance when you can expect the peaks and valleys of student interest allows the astute director to head off any loss of momentum. A well-timed activity can almost always counteract a waning of student interest. Most elementary directors would agree with the following assessment of the year's high and low points.

PREPARE FOR THE PREDICTABLE SLUMP IN INTEREST

The first month is a director's dream. Enthusiasm is so high that the students practice without being reminded. They all remember to bring their instruments and books to class and they arrive on time. Everyone turns in a practice card and the recorded practice times are fantastic. Progress occurs by leaps and bounds, and both students and their parents can easily see the achievement. This is the time to carefully establish routines, to maintain consistency and to work primarily in the method book, setting a solid foundation for learning during the remainder of the year.

After the initial month or two, the novelty wears off and students tend to slack off in their practice; the second month or so would be a good time to introduce a new activity. Issuing a challenge to the students is one possibility—i.e., "Whoever can play this song perfectly next week will win a prize." Then be sure to have plenty of prizes on hand the following week. I stock up on prize items whenever I find a bargain. Pencils or erasers with a music theme make good prizes. The thought of winning something can be a great motivator.

Planning a small-scale performance can also motivate students. Once beginners have learned a few familiar tunes, they want to perform them for anyone who will listen. *Hot Crossed Buns, Mary Had a Little Lamb,* and *Twinkle, Twinkle Little Star* are favorites. You might say, "Next week we'll go to the kindergarten rooms to play for the students. Everyone remember your instrument and practice hard this week." You can build the performance into as big an event as you wish, choosing students to tell a little about their instruments or about the band. Students may want to dress a certain way (i.e., uniform colors or clothes with a theme), or they may have ideas about the presentation. Listen to their suggestions and learn—they know what appeals to children. Although you may tire of doing this with every class, all of your students will want their classes to perform. Try to make arrangements with the lower-grade teachers, the cafeteria hostess, and the office staff so that your groups can play for different audiences. Remember that those kindergartners and first and second graders will soon be fifth graders who are eligible for the band. The seeds you plant today you will reap in a few years. These performances not only benefit your current band in fostering pride and motivation, but will also benefit your future band program, serving as a pre-recruitment. Make the most of the opportunity.

Introducing sheet music to beginners for the first time can be another fantastic motivator. Once the basics of sound production, hand position, and note reading are mastered and the students have learned about six notes, they are ready to try sheet music. I generally save this activity for the first week back after Thanksgiving. Returning from a break can be a low point for students, and introducing sheet music is a perfect morale booster. I begin with a simple band arrangement of *Jingle Bells*. Even though this tune is in most method books, the fact that it is printed on a separate sheet seems to be significant to children. The arrangement that I use has the melody with either a duet or a trio part on each sheet, so everyone can play the melody at home, and the teacher can have students try various parts in school. The director can easily arrange familiar tunes in three- or four-part harmony, and the parts can be tailored to your students. Any beginning band piece will do, however, as long as it is geared to the level of your students. Watch particularly for oboe parts and French horn parts which are often in a poor range for beginners—you may need to revise the parts.

The three to four weeks between Thanksgiving and Christmas provide a great opportunity to reinvigorate students, and the timing is crucial. Many music stores offer an initial three-month instrument rental contract at a low price as a trial period for the student. Thereafter, the instrument is rented by the month at a slightly higher rate. Because beginners usually start band around the beginning of October or late September (after all the recruitment programs, parent meetings, and time to obtain instruments), their trial period expires around Christmas. Likewise, school-owned instruments are rented by the semester, and most directors hand out new contracts in January. Rather than having the child make a year long commitment to play in the band, many parents view it as a three-month commitment, at which point they will assess the situation and decide on their child's future participation. That makes the Christmas/winter vacation a crucial time. If parents see students losing interest, they will be likely to discontinue. Unless student interest is maintained, the band director could return in January from the winter break to find that many students' instruments have been returned to the music stores. For this reason it is paramount that the students leave for their break motivated to continue.

The ideal solution to the problem of motivation is to schedule a winter concert for one of the last days before the break. A school assembly program is the perfect forum. All band students perform together on several pieces, and the advanced students then play a few tunes on their own. Children love to play for their peers and teachers; my students get so excited about performing that the gym seems to be charged with energy. I know of no better student motivator than such a performance. Scheduling an evening concert for parents is an additional idea. It is important for the parents to see the result of their child's efforts. The holidays are such a busy time that some directors wait and schedule a parent concert in January or February. On the positive side, this can raise morale during what is probably the biggest lull in the school year; on the negative side, holiday tunes which may have been included on the school concert are no longer appropriate, so students must prepare new pieces.

Preparing for concerts does slow progress in the method book, so I try to move along as far as possible in the book before the first concert. Once your students move away from the book, it is difficult to make them go back— once they have sampled band music, they will want to continue with that.

The waning of interest in January and February can be frustrating. Preparing for a special concert, perhaps for Valentine's Day, is one way to overcome the doldrums. I begin talking about the solo and ensemble festival and distributing music as soon as we return from the winter break. Students are excited by the possibility of winning medals and are anxious to practice a solo or ensemble. January may seem early to begin preparations when the festival is in April, but you will need the time to help students prepare and to avoid a rush at the last minute. I also begin passing out sheet music that I might want to have the students perform in the spring concert. This keeps everyone looking ahead. Continue games, playing for prizes, and impromptu performances in class.

If the area band will attend the district band festival in March, this becomes an intense time of preparation. I find this to be very motivating for my advanced students. Most have never attended a band festival before and are looking forward to the event.

March is officially MENC's "Music in the Schools Month" and is a good time to promote music in your school; while you are at it, you can also motivate students. Have a poster contest for band students, give a lunch-time recital, decorate a display case, or perform at a retirement home. The possibilities are endless. Continue to pass out new music in preparation for the spring concert.

The end-of-the-year stretch usually begins in April. The solo and ensemble festival is the high point of this month. The more students you involve, the more your band is motivated. I often take entire classes to the festival as large ensembles. Class time is used to prepare for the event, and the students feel that they are working toward a common goal. Preparing for the festival fosters a sense of camaraderie among the band students. All are anxious to win medals and are strongly motivated. Even those who do not participate can be caught up in the excitement of preparing for the event. A recital prior to the festival adds to the excitement and provides a test run for the students attending the festival. With spring break usually occurring sometime in April, these two events seem to fill up the month and keep everyone busy.

Momentum climbs higher still in May as the spring concert nears. Students look forward to full rehearsals, and I try to schedule about five of them prior to the concert. I often invite people in to hear the rehearsal, and this can add to the excitement of a rehearsal. I like to schedule the big concert for the end of May. That leaves June to devote to special events such as field day and the school picnic. Often the intermediate director wishes to hear sixth graders audition for placement in next year's band during the month of June. Each school has its own special activities in June, and the resourceful band director can keep student interest at its peak right up to the end of the year by involving the band in the activities. I pass out summer band letters just before the spring concert when enthusiasm is high. Shortly after the concert, I can usually count on receiving many summer band registration forms. The students are so excited from the concert that they are eager to continue playing in a band over the summer. The spring concert is such a strong motivator that the students' enthusiasm carries over through the summer.

With foresight and planning, the wise director can ensure that student interest is maintained at a high level throughout the year. Knowing the predictable pattern of waxing and waning student interest, and counteracting the waning periods with special activities and music are important tasks of the elementary director.

Finally, it is important to respond promptly at the first sign of a student's falling behind. Whether it is due to illness, a broken instrument, lack of practice, or lack of talent, once students fall behind, they are heading toward dropping out. Nothing is more frustrating and embarrassing to a child than to be the only one in a group who can't do something correctly. The easy solution is to give up. As soon as I think that there may be a problem, I try to give that student extra help, either during or after school. Contact with the parents is important to ensure that the student practices and has support at home. Sometimes it may take weeks of extra help, and sometimes I may need to move the student to a more individualized setting with fewer students. I hate to lose any players regardless of talent, and I do whatever I can to ensure success for all who join the band.

Some students learn more slowly than others and can greatly benefit from private lessons. Most band teachers do not have enough time during the day to devote to teaching individual students. Recommending a private teacher is a wise move. The high school band director can also recommend any high school students who are interested in teaching. The use of a student tutor often appeals to parents for several reasons: the high school students are less expensive, are closer to the child's age and therefore may be better able to communicate, may even come to the house, and can provide an enlightening and motivating glimpse into the world of high school band. Even advanced elementary students can help a slower beginner. Whatever the approach, prompt remedial action is necessary if the student's interest is to be maintained.

RESPOND PROMPTLY WHEN STUDENTS FALL BEHIND

In conclusion, maintaining a high level of student interest throughout the year is a challenge and one of the most important tasks of an elementary band director. It is normal for student interest to decline after the novelty of learning an instrument wears off; however, the enterprising band director will be able to regenerate interest during the course of the year. Having students perform often, maintaining a regular schedule, keeping the band and oneself in the public eye, providing special activities, selecting appropriate music, preparing for the inevitable lulls, and reacting promptly when students fall behind are some ideas for maintaining interest. ■

CONCLUSION

Guide To Solo And Ensemble Music

The annual solo and ensemble festival can be an elementary band director's worst headache or an enjoyable and worthwhile experience for students and teacher alike. In the past, the solo festival was considered by many to be an activity for intermediate and high school students, specifically, those taking private lessons; however, more recently, the solo festival has become as much an elementary band event as it is an upper grade event. When the majority of participating students were those studying privately, the school band director had limited involvement, other than submitting the required paperwork and maintaining membership in the state music association—the private teacher handled the music selection and preparation. In contrast, the participation of elementary students generally requires major involvement and committment on the part of the band teacher. The payoff, in terms of student motivation and progress, is worth the effort.

While some elementary students have private teachers who can help them prepare for a festival, most do not; the band teacher must not only help the remaining students prepare their solos, but must also select the music to be performed. The process of music selection can be extremely time-consuming for one who is unfamiliar with the solo literature at the elementary level—it takes hours or days to study the available music, assuming that you can find a store with a good stock of solo literature. This research must be done early in the year so that solos can be ordered and will arrive well before the festival.

There are several resources available to help directors in selecting solo and ensemble music. The Virginia Band and Orchestra Directors' Association (VBODA) manual (or its equivalent in other states) is a comprehensive listing of solo and ensemble music, classified by instrument and grade; however, I do not recommend ordering music, sight unseen, based on title alone or on its inclusion in a manual. There is great variance in difficulty among pieces listed under the same grade level, and the solos are often more difficult or easier than one might expect. The *Director's Guide to Festival and Contest Music*, published by *The Instrumentalist*, is another useful resource, as are reviews in *The Instrumentalist* and other publications.

The following list of recommended solos and ensembles is included to aid the elementary band director in selecting appropriate music for students. The difficulty level of the music is indicated by numbers corresponding to years of study: "1" would be suitable for an average first-year student, "2" for a second-year student, and so forth. Plusses after the number designations indicate a slightly higher degree of difficulty. All of these pieces have been enjoyed by my students and are my personal favorites; however, there are many other fine pieces available, and I recommend taking the time, when you can find it, to study the available literature.

Flute Solos

(1)   *Echo Song*, Ralph Guenther (Belwin)

(1)   *When the Saints Go Marching In*, arr. Forrest Buchtel (Kjos)

(1)   *Serenade*, Mozart/arr. Forrest Buchtel (Kjos)

(1)   *March for Flutists*, Ralph Guenther (Belwin)

(1+) *Yankee Dandy*, Ralph Guenther (Belwin)

(1+) *Minuet in G*, Bach/Arr. Forrest Buchtel (Kjos)

(2)   *Glow Worm*, Lincke/Forrest Buchtel (Kjos)

(2)   *Polovetsian Dances*, Borodin/arr. Forrest Buchtel (Kjos)

(2)   *Fiesta*, William Billingsley (Belwin)

(2)   *Spanish Folk Song*, Ralph Guenther (Belwin)

(2)   *Celebrated Gavotte*, Martini/arr. Forrest Buchtel (Kjos)

(2+) *The Entertainer*, Joplin/arr. Forrest Buchtel (Kjos)

Flute Ensembles

(1-2) *Learn to Play Flute Duets*, comp./ed./arr. William Eisenhauer (Alfred)

(2+) *Menuet and Trio* (quartet), Schubert/arr. Clair W. Johnson (Rubank)

Oboe Solos

(1) *Humming Song*, Schumann/arr. Arthur Best (Belwin)

(1) *Gypsy Sweetheart*, arr. Arthur Best (Belwin)

(1+) *Scarborough Fair*, arr. Robert Foster (Belwin)

(2) *Caprice*, Blaine Edlefsen (Belwin)

(2) *Allegretto*, Blaine Edlefsen (Belwin)

(2) *To a Wild Rose*, arr. Blaine Edlefsen (Belwin)

(2) *Prelude and Dance*, Frank Erickson/ed. Arthur Best (Belwin)

Clarinet Solos

(1) *Little Piece*, Schumann/arr. Frank Erickson/ed. David Shifrin (Belwin)

(1) *Janus*, Forrest Buchtel (Kjos)

(1) *Il Primo Canto*, Nilo Hovey and Beldon Leonard (Belwin)

(1) *Caissons Go Rolling Along*, arr. Forrest Buchtel (Kjos)

(1) *Menuet in G*, Bach/trans. Dishinger (Medici)

(1) *Waltz Miniature*, arr. Nilo Hovey and Beldon Leonard (Belwin)

(1) *March of the Dwarfs*, Jack End (Kendor)

(1+) *Aria and Scherzo*, Frank Erickson/ed. David Shifrin (Belwin)

(1+) *Skater's Waltz*, E. Waldteuffel/arr. Art Jolliff (Rubank)

(2) *King's Jester Waltz*, Forrest Buchtel (Kjos)

(2) *Minuet in G*, Bach/arr. Forrest Buchtel (Kjos)

(2+) *Celebrated Gavotte*, Martini/arr. Forrest Buchtel (Kjos)

(2+) *Gavotte*, Gossec/arr. Fred Weber (Belwin)

Clarinet Ensembles

(1-2) *Learn to Play Clarinet Duets*, comp./ed./arr. William Eisenhauer (Alfred)

(2) *Menuet in G (quartet)*, Bach/arr. Ronald Dishinger (Medici)

Bass Clarinet

(1+) *The Happy Hippo*, Neal Porter (Belwin)

(2) *Boogie Bass*, Norman Goldberg (Belwin)

(2) *Polka*, von Suppe/arr. Neal Porter (Belwin)

Alto Saxophone

(1) *Little Folk Song*, Robert Foster (Belwin)

(1) *Caissons Go Rolling Along*, arr. Forrest Buchtel (Kjos)

(1) *Fox You Stole the Goose*, Sigurd Rascher (Belwin)

(1+) *American Folk Tune*, arr. Sigurd Rascher (Belwin)

(2) *Jiggle a Bit*, Forrest Buchtel (Kjos)

(2+) *Aria*, Willis Coggins (Belwin)

(2+) *The Entertainer*, Joplin/arr. Forrest Buchtel (Kjos)

Saxophone Ensembles

(2) *Amigos (duet)*, Richard Fote (Kendor)

Tenor Saxophone

(1) *Tenor Touchdown*, Eugene Rousseau (Belwin)

(2) *Menuet in G*, Bach/Ronald Dishinger (Medici)

(2) *Gavotte*, Corelli/Willis Coggins (Belwin)

Trumpet

(1) *Caissons Go Rolling Along*, arr. Forrest Buchtel (Kjos)

(1+) *Marine's Hymn*, Phillips/arr. Forrest Buchtel (Kjos)

(1) *Neophyte*, Leonard Smith (Belwin)

(2) *Happy Bugler*, Forrest Buchtel (Kjos)

(2) *Rigaudon from "Pieces de Clavecin,"* Rameau/trans. Ronald Dishinger (Medici)

(2) *Golden Glow*, Leonard Smith (Belwin)

(2) *Celebrated Gavotte*, Martini/arr. Forrest Buchtel (Kjos)

(2+) *Trumpet Voluntary*, Purcell/arr. Bobby Herriot (Belwin)

(2+) *The Entertainer*, Joplin/arr. Forrest Buchtel (Kjos)

Trumpet Ensembles

(2) *Amigos (duet)*, Richard Fote (Kendor)

(1-2) *Learn to Play Cornet Duets*, comp./ed./arr. William Eisenhauer (Alfred)

Mixed Brass Ensembles

(2+) *Scherzando* (for 2 tpts. and 2 trombones—opt. F horn and Bar. T.C. may sub. for trombones) Reichardt/arr. Frank Erickson (Belwin)

French Horn

(1) *Hymn to Joy*, Beethoven/arr. Forsberg (Belwin)

(1-) *French Child's Song*, Behr/arr. James Ployhar (Belwin)

(1+) *Our Favorite*, Leonard Smith (Belwin)

(1+) *Nobility*, Leonard Smith (Belwin)

(2) *Rigaudon from "Pieces de Clavecin,"* Rameau/trans. Ronald Dishinger (Medici)

(2+) *The Hunt*, James Ployhar (Belwin)

French Horn Ensembles

    (1-2) *Ode to Joy (quartet)*, Beethoven/arr. James Ployhar (Belwin)

Trombone

    (1)   *Indian Song*, Leonard Smith (Belwin)

    (1)   *Caissons Go Rolling Along*, arr. Forrest Buchtel (Kjos)

    (1+)   *Marine's Hymn*, Phillips/arr. Forrest Buchtel (Kjos)

    (1+)   *Military March*, arr. Donald Little (Belwin)

    (2+)   *Hot Taco*, Paul Tanner (Belwin)

Baritone

    (1)   *Caissons Go Rolling Along*, arr. Forrest Buchtel (Kjos)

    (1)   *Cheyenne*, Leonard Smith (Belwin)

    (1+)   *Marine's Hymn*, Phillips/arr. Forrest Buchtel (Kjos)

    (1+)   *Military March*, arr. Donald Little (Belwin)

    (1+)   *Cactus Jack*, Leonard Smith (Belwin)

    (2)   *Wagons Roll*, Paul Tanner (Belwin)

    (2)   *Baritone Bacarat*, Paul Tanner (Belwin)

    (2+)   *Las Tortillas*, Paul Tanner (Belwin)

Tuba

    (1)   *King Neptune*, Acton Ostling (Belwin)

    (1)   *Bicycle Built for Two*, Dacre/arr. Donald Little (Belwin)

    (1+)   *Old American Patriotic Song*, Billings/arr. James Barnes (Belwin)

    (1+)   *Military March*, arr. Donald Little (Belwin)

    (2+)   *Haydn Medley (from Symphony No. 94)*, arr. William Bell (Belwin)

Bells

    (1)   *Andante Theme*, Haydn/arr. Acton Ostling (Belwin)

    (1)   *A Walk Through Kalamazoo*, Wally Barnett (Belwin)

    (2+)   *High School Cadets*, Sousa/arr. Wally Barnett (Belwin)

    (2+)   *Our Director*, Bigelow/arr. Sandy Feldstein (Belwin)

Snare Drum

    (1)   *Caissons Go Rolling Along*, arr. Forrest Buchtel (Kjos)

    (1+)   *American Patrol*, Martini/arr. Forrest Buchtel (Kjos)

    (2)   *Aquamarine* (unaccompanied)   Haskell Harr (Belwin)

    (2)   *Marines' Hymn*, Phillips/arr. Forrest Buchtel (Kjos)

Percussion Ensembles

(1)   *Percussion Ensembles for Young Performers*, John Kinyon (Alfred)

(1+2+) *Alfred's Learn to Play Snare Drum Duets*, Sandy Feldstein and Dave Black (Alfred)

(2)   *Jive for Five*, Wally Barnett (Belwin)

(3+)   *Interplay (sextet)*, Garwood Whaley (Meredith)

Suggested Ensemble Books

Alfred's Basic Band Solos and Ensembles, Books 1 and 2 (Alfred)
    (Specify instrument when ordering. Can be used with any combination of instruments. Contains solos, duet, and trios.)

Yamaha Band Ensembles, Books 1 and 2 (Yamaha)
    (Trio arrangements. Can be used with any combination of instruments)

Woodwind Ensembles for Young Performers, John Kinyon (Alfred)
    (Trio arrangements for one flute and two clarinets)

Brass Ensembles for Young Performers, John Kinyon (Alfred)
    (Trio arrangements for mixed brasses)

Trios for All, Stoutamire and Henderson, (Pro Art) ∎

BAND!!

Dear Parent: 9/10/*00*

Your fifth or sixth grade child is invited to participate in the Cherry Run Elementary School band program! Fairfax County Public Schools provide free class instruction to all interested fifth and sixth grade students on flute, oboe, clarinet, saxophone, trumpet, French horn, trombone, baritone, tuba, or percussion. Band classes meet once a week during the regular school day and are open to students at all levels of proficiency, including the beginning level.

Participating in the school band program is fun and rewarding for students. Our Cherry Run band performs several times during the year and is an integral part of the school. Students may continue in band at the intermediate and high school levels where there are opportunities to participate in many exciting school, area, and state bands. Credit toward graduation is earned by high school students who participate in the school band.

Instruments are to be supplied by the students; our local music stores offer excellent rental/purchase plans. A limited number of instruments are available for student rental through Cherry Run Elementary School. Books and music will be provided by the school.

Interested parents and students are invited to attend an informational meeting on Thursday, September 17, at 7:30 PM in the Cherry Run gym. Instruments will be available for examination, and I will answer any questions which you may have concerning the school band program. I will assist parents and students in selecting an enjoyable and suitable instrument for the student. If you are unable to attend the meeting, or if you have any questions, please feel free to contact me at Cherry Run School.

Sincerely,

Mrs. Eileen Fraedrich
Cherry Run School
(add phone number)

Cherry Run Elementary School Band

What instrument would you like to play? Write a *1* for 1st choice, a *2* for 2nd choice, and a *3* for 3rd choice.

_____ flute	_____ French horn
_____ oboe	_____ trombone
_____ clarinet	_____ baritone
_____ saxophone	_____ tuba
_____ trumpet	_____ percussion

Student's Name _____ Grade _____

Classroom Teacher _____

Home Address _____

_____

Phone _____

Parent's Signature _____

Work Phone _____

☐ - I would like to join the Cherry Run Band.

☐ - I was in band last year and wish to continue this year.

Please return this form to your classroom teacher by Monday, September 21.

BAND INFORMATIONAL MEETING!!

9/10/*00*

For parents of students interested in beginning a band instrument this year!

DATE: Wednesday, September 15

TIME: 7:30-8:30 PM

PLACE: Cherry Run—cafeteria

Students will be attending an instrument demonstration assembly on Monday, September 13, and will receive informational letters at that time. If you are unable to attend the parents' meeting, but have questions, feel free to contact me at Cherry Run (*add phone number*). I will also be at Back-to-School Night on Monday, September 20.

I look forward to teaching your children!

Eileen Fraedrich
Band Director
Cherry Run School

WELCOME TO THE CHERRY RUN BAND!!!

Students should have the following equipment for band class:

Flute - cleaning rod and cloth

Oboe - 1 plastic reed (medium-soft) or 2 cane reeds (1 soft and 1 medium-soft), a cleaning swab, cork grease

Clarinet - at least 6 reeds (number 2 or medium-soft), a cleaning swab, cork grease

Saxophone - at least 6 reeds (number 2 to 2½, or medium-soft), cork grease, a cleaning swab, neck strap

Trumpet - valve oil*, mouthpiece brush, a soft cloth

French Horn - valve oil*, mouthpiece brush, a soft cloth

Trombone - slide oil*, mouthpiece brush, a soft cloth

Baritone - valve oil*, mouthpiece brush, a soft cloth

Tuba - valve oil*, mouthpiece brush, a soft cloth

Percussion - a bell/drum kit with drum pad and stand, 2B or 2S sticks, a 2½ octave set of bells with stand, bell mallets

* I recommend a non-toxic oil, such as Space Filler™ brand, which the students can bring to school.

A folding music stand for home practice is recommended, but optional.

Please try to have instruments and accessories by Monday, September 27. If you have any questions, please contact me at Cherry Run Elementary School (*add phone number*).

Eileen Fraedrich
Band Director

APPENDIX D:
Sample
Practice Cards

Practice Card ♪	Practice Card ♪
Name_____	Name_____
Date_____	Date_____
Monday_____	Monday_____
Tuesday_____	Tuesday_____
Wednesday_____	Wednesday_____
Thursday_____	Thursday_____
Friday_____	Friday_____
Saturday_____	Saturday_____
Sunday_____	Sunday_____
TOTAL_____	TOTAL_____
Parent's Signature_____	Parent's Signature_____
Assignment for Next Week:	Assignment for Next Week:
_____	_____
_____	_____

NOTE-READING GAME

(In the blanks, write the letter names of the notes to spell words)

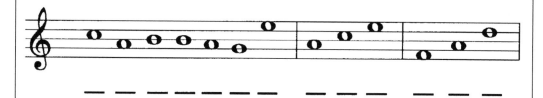

APPENDIX F:
Sample
Concert
Program
(outside)

The Cherry Run Band

presents

Spring Concert 0000

Lake Braddock Secondary School—Theater
May 13, 0000
7:30 PM

BAND STUDENTS

Tenor Saxophone

Trumpet

Trombone

Baritone

Tuba

Percussion

French Horn

APPENDIX F:
Sample
Concert
Program
(inside)

Program

Cherry Run March .... Fraedrich

Anasazi .... Edmondson

Band on Parade .... Sebesky

Theme from Beethoven's Ninth Symphony .... Beethoven/ Arr. Tyler

The Blue Rock .... Lauder

The Silver Scepter .... Kinyon

Ten Little Drummers .... Balent

Let's Go Band .... Balent

* *

Eileen Fraedrich, Director

Dr. Mary Smith, Principal
Dr. Susan Jones, Assistant Principal

BAND STUDENTS

Piccolo

Flute

(List names)

Oboe

Clarinet

Bass Clarinet

Soprano Saxophone

Alto Saxophone

CHERRY RUN BAND - SPRING CONCERT

4/26/*00*

Dear Band Parents,

Our spring concert is fast approaching, and it promises to be an exciting event. The students have done an excellent job of preparing their music, and our rehearsals have gone well!! We are looking forward to performing on the stage at Lake Braddock. Please make a note of the following important concert information:

DATE: Thursday, May 13, *0000*
PLACE: Lake Braddock Secondary School - theater
(Students report to room J104—band room, across from theater)

TIME: 7:30 PM (Students report at 7:00 PM)

DRESS: Boys - dark slacks, white shirt, tie
Girls - dark skirt, white blouse

EQUIPMENT: Instrument, music, music stand (if you have one)

In preparation for the concert, we will be having two more full band rehearsals which will take the place of regularly scheduled band classes. The following is our band rehearsal schedule:
Tuesday, May 4
Tuesday, May 11

* Students are reminded to bring instruments, music, and music stands (if they have them) to each rehearsal.

I am anticipating an excellent concert!!

Sincerely,
Eileen Fraedrich

(Please detach and return by Monday, May 5)

- -

 4/26/*00*

_____
Student's name

I have received the spring concert information letter and my son/daughter will be present for the event. I will arrange for my child's transportation.

_____
Parent's signature

A few parents are needed to assist with transporting equipment and setting up at Lake

Braddock beginning around 4:30 PM. If you are able to help, please check here:_____.

WINTER ASSEMBLY CONCERTS MONDAY MORNING!!

12/15/00

Dear Band Students and Parents,

Our winter assembly concerts are scheduled for next Monday morning, December 20! All 155 band students will be playing together for the first time, which should be very exciting! The following concert information applies:

TIME: 9:15 AM Check in with classroom teacher and report to gym.

10:00 AM Lower grade assembly concert

10:45 AM Upper grade assembly concert

DRESS: School colors—red and white. Everyday clothes are fine.

EQUIPMENT: Instrument, music, music stand (if you have one)

Parents are welcome to attend.

Practice hard this weekend! I'm looking forward to a fun concert on Monday!

BURKE AREA BAND

Terra Centre/Cherry Run/Bonnie Brae/Fairview

October 12, *0000*

Dear Band Students and Parents,

The Burke Area Band is an outstanding elementary level musical ensemble which is comprised of advanced band students from several schools in our area. The group rehearses on a weekly basis. Students who participate in the band benefit from the experience of performing in a large, full band setting with other advanced students.

Auditions for the Burke Area Band will begin the week of October 18 (Oct. 12 at Terra Centre and Bonnie Brae) during band class. Any advanced band member may audition. Band rehearsals will be held on Mondays at Robinson Secondary School from 2:45 PM to 4:00 PM. Rehearsals will begin on Monday, November 8. Beginning in January, there will be a second rehearsal each week in preparation for the district festival in March. The additional rehearsals will be scheduled for either Wednesday or Thursday evenings (to be announced at our first band rehearsal) and will continue through the beginning of March.

If the band works hard and is well-prepared, we will participate in the following activities:

Winter Concert - December
Pre-Festival Concert - February or March
District Festival - March
Spring Tour - a concert tour of several elementary schools during May.
Spring Concert - May

Auditions will include:

1) Scales played from memory:
Flutes, Oboes, Trombones, Baritones, Tubas—B flat and F major scales
Clarinets, Tenor Saxophones, Trumpets—C and G major scales
Alto Saxophones—G and D major scales
French Horns—F and C major scales
Bells—B flat and C major scales (also a closed roll on snare drum)

2) A prepared piece (to be announced in band class). This music does not need to be memorized.

Students who do not pass the audition but have shown a positive attitude and a willingness to work may be placed in the Area Band on a trial basis. I will be happy to help anyone who would like extra help on this or on any other band assignment. Please see me to arrange a time if you would like help.

Mrs. Fraedrich—Cherry Run Elementary

BURKE AREA BAND

October 25, *0000*

Dear Band Parents,

_____ has auditioned for and has been accepted as a member of the Burke Area Band. This year's band promises to be an outstanding elementary level musical ensemble. We are excited to be working with such a talented group of students.

The area band will rehearse on Mondays, beginning November 8, in the intermediate band room at Robinson Secondary School. Rehearsals will be from 2:45 PM to 4:00 PM. Beginning in January and continuing until early March, there will be a second rehearsal each week, on either Wednesday or Thursday evenings (to be announced). Attendance at rehearsals is necessary if the band is to accomplish its performance goals for the year. Students who are involved in other activities which regularly conflict with area band rehearsals (baseball, soccer, Scouts, etc.) should decide which activities they will pursue. A winter concert in December, a pre-festival concert in February or March, a festival performance in March, a spring tour in May, and a spring concert in either April or May are planned.

Students should remember to bring pencils to all rehearsals. Monday rehearsals will end at 4:00 PM. Please try to be prompt in picking up children following rehearsals. Car pools have worked well in the past; if you would like to be included on a car pool list to be given to interested area band students, please complete the bottom portion of this form.

I am looking forward to starting rehearsals on November 8 and to preparing for our upcoming winter concert!

Sincerely,

Mrs. Fraedrich

- -

Please complete this section if you wish the information to be included on a car pool list.

_____   _____

Student's name   Phone number

_____

Address

APPENDIX K:
Sample
Solo and
Ensemble
Recital
Letter

SOLO AND ENSEMBLE PRE-FESTIVAL RECITAL!!

4/12/00

Dear Parents and Students,

In preparation for the upcoming Solo and Ensemble Festival to be held on Saturday, April 24, we will have an optional pre-festival recital at Cherry Run for parents and students! The recital will be held on Thursday, April 22, beginning at 7:30 PM in the Cherry Run cafeteria. If you would like to perform on the recital, please return the attached form by Monday, April 19. Please remember to check with your accompanist before responding. Dress clothes should be worn.

There will be a reception following the recital; if you are able to bring a refreshment, please indicate this on the detach and return section. The recital should provide an excellent opportunity for students to prepare for their festival performances that weekend. I hope that all students who are attending the Solo and Ensemble Festival will want to participate. I am looking forward to an exciting recital!

Sincerely,

Eileen Fraedrich - band

- - - - - - - - - - (Please detach and return by Monday, April 19) - - - - - - - - - -

_____   _____
Student's name   Accompanist

_____
Title and Composer of Solo/Ensemble

If you will bring a refreshment, please check below:

_____ I will bring a beverage (2 liter bottle of soda)

_____ I will bring cookies, brownies, etc.

_____
Parent's signature

APPENDIX L:
Sample
Solo and
Ensemble
Recital
Program

RECITAL

Thursday April 22, *0000*

The Earle of Oxford's Marche .... Byrd
Arr. Dishinger

(Student's Name Here)
(Accompanist's name here)

Amigos .... Fote
(Student's Name Here)
(Accompanist's name here)

Minuet in G .... Bach
(Student's Name Here)
(Accompanist's name here)

Allegro .... Suzuki
(Student's Name Here)
(Accompanist's name here)

The Happy Bugler .... Buchtel
(Student's Name Here)
(Accompanist's name here)

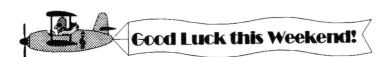

Good Luck this Weekend!

ABOUT THE AUTHOR...

Eileen Fraedrich has taught band in Fairfax County, Virginia, since 1984. She graduated as valedictorian from Mount Vernon High School in Fairfax County, received her Bachelor of Music Degree, *summa cum laude*, from Ithaca College, Ithaca, New York, and received her Master of Arts Degree from George Mason University, Fairfax, Virginia. A 1991 Teacher of the Year Nominee, she served as secretary of the Fairfax County Band Directors' Association for many years and has been a presenter at educational conferences and workshops. Her elementary bands are recognized for their high levels of student participation and musical achievement.